IT'S NEVER ABOUT THE MONEY

Frank McCarthy

Published by OAK TREE PRESS
19 Rutland Street, Cork, Ireland
www.oaktreepress.com / www.SuccessStore.com
www.itsneveraboutthemoney.com

A catalogue record of this book is available from the British Library.

ISBN 978 1 78119 156 9 (paperback)
ISBN 978 1 78119 157 6 (ePub)
ISBN 978 1 78119 158 3 (Kindle)

Cover image by Brian Byrne
Cover design by Kieran O'Connor Design

Printed in Ireland by SPRINT-print Ltd.

CONTENTS

DEDICATION

It's never easy to write a book. Whether they like it or not, your immediate family are punished the entire time it takes. Hearing the rejected paragraphs hit the waste bin, signalling another cup of tea, must be very trying. Each played their part.

My wife Sinead's attitude of "I will back you no matter what" made any fear of failure dissipate and gave me the foundation I needed. My 12 year old daughter, Amy, and her tough love approach was an everyday motivation. My 13 year old daughter, Meg, made a great contribution: taking the cover design and etching the word "think" into the roots of the tree, further ensuring readers get the message. And finally, Rob, my son, who left me in peace with his "I will get in the picture with you when you are famous" silent message.

So this part of the journey is over.

This book is for all of you.

Thank You.

Frank McCarthy
Dublin
January 2015

ACKNOWLEDGEMENTS

Entrepreneur and solicitor, **Noel Smyth**, for his time and effort in reading this book – and for his stern insistence that I publish it.

Entrepreneur **Dermot Desmond**, for his *Foreword* and his immediate quick response and careful, honest assessment of the book.

Entrepreneur **Denis O'Brien**, for helping this book happen and pushing all he could in every way he could to see it published.

Tom Bartlett, an author himself, from the outset giving hours (or was it months?) of time and effort in making suggestions and corrections, pushing timelines and, in many ways, babysitting the author.

Rita O'Kane, the wise wife of my publisher, for taking *It's Never About the Money* out of her husband's 'not to print' bin and insisting it be published. What a judge Rita is!

FOREWORD

I have just one issue with this book: the title, ***It's Never About The Money***. As a financier, I know that the only way to survive in business is to have a positive profit and loss statement. Having said that, I completely understand what Frank McCarthy means – it's about the person who leads and how they treat and interact with those they work and socialise with.

Frank considers the biggest obstacle to entrepreneurship to be fear. This reminds me of the saying:

> *Courage is not about freedom from fear but about being afraid and going on.*

There is no doubt that Frank is an entrepreneur. From the age of eight, he was selling bundles of sticks for firelighters by collecting old wood from building sites. This commercial initiative, as he says in this book, has been successfully replicated in different forms throughout his business life.

It's Never About the Money is the accumulation of the knowledge that he learnt from working in the British Leyland assembly plant, to being one of Ireland's first photocopier salesmen, to establishing his building services business. It demonstrates why he is such a natural entrepreneur, with a gift for recognising opportunities in the fast-moving world we live in now.

Another hallmark of Frank McCarthy and his business acumen is encompassed in the adage that:

Nobody ever went broke by taking a profit.

An underlying vein throughout the book is Frank's ability to understand the psychology of his fellow-workers, which is best illustrated when he makes the profound comment:

> *When people see themselves as separate to the company, then they have no problem damaging the company, or running it down. This is a difficult lesson to swallow, but one that every entrepreneur must remember. Teach your employees and get them to understand that they are the business.*

Throughout the book, Frank's key message is that it is not the business that makes money, it is the people who operate the business who determine whether it succeeds or fails.

Further good advice is not to listen to the naysayers. They will say: "It is too difficult; you will never get funding; you don't have the skill set; it's been tried before and failed". I could not agree more. Surround yourself with positivity and honest critics (mothers are best!). If you believe in the opportunity, don't allow anyone to build up your fears, just because they are afraid of their own inadequacies. Instead, take that extra step which always has an element of risk, otherwise courage from fear would not be required.

Frank recounts lots of funny experiences and anecdotes of how he earned his 'Master's' in business. However, I think that when you read the book, you will recognise that he deserves a PhD in wisdom!

Dermot F Desmond

There are so many myths about entrepreneurs that it is difficult for anyone to fathom what actually spurs people. Frank McCarthy's book is a great read, primarily because it demystifies these myths. "Hard worker, early starter, willing to be free, to take chances, to live your life, these are the key attributes of an entrepreneur", he writes. I would add 'is the master of your own life'.

But if you aspire to be an entrepreneur, there is one trait that you need to have more than anything else – the willingness to work brutally hard.

Another is being able to face failure. And, unfortunately, that sometimes means actually failing. Business failure at an early stage spurred me on – and does so still to this day.

We all recall that first bicycle ride, especially the falling off part! But the determination to get back on the bike with bruised knee and battered ego is what matters most. Then there is the exhilaration of the wind blowing in your face as you freewheel down the road, having got back on the saddle. The road of life is no different.

Much of entrepreneurship is seeing the positive from the negative. One person might see a problem about which nothing can be done. The entrepreneur thinks differently and asks "Where is the opportunity in the problem?".

I can readily identify with this book because it takes the reader through all the stages of being a self-starter. Frank recalls chopping and selling painted wood, which burned better, as an eight year old. That was his first business venture – seeing an opportunity and converting it into cash.

I hope many young women and men interested in business read *It's Never About The Money*. They will learn so much. It's a great read and I hope you enjoy it.

Denis O'Brien

1: A CALL TO ARMS

I am an entrepreneur. You are an entrepreneur too.

Accountants, naysayers, lazybones, professionals, oxygen-stealers, experts, consultants – we are surrounded by them our whole lives. They are our enemies. They are our obstacles.

Do you feel trapped? Do you wonder what is going on around you? Do you feel out of place?

You need to believe you can do better. You must understand your life is not over yet. Please realise you are not alone.

Are you ready now? Has life convinced you it is finally time to take matters into your own hands? Are you surrounded by the lazy, the deluded and the restricted?

Do you want to think for yourself? Do you want to use your own mind, to have your own thoughts?

You need to do more than simply decide. You have to have the talk with yourself. What is the talk? The talk is self-talk. It is when you have a question and answer session with yourself. Here is a simple example: "Will I have lunch now, or will I wait? Yeah, I will wait".

Who has just answered you? There must be two to talk: yourself the speaker and yourself the listener.

"Do I want to be an entrepreneur, or don't I?", this is the question you must ask yourself.

If you can make up your own mind, think for yourself and maybe allow yourself to make a mistake or two, then you can be an entrepreneur in whatever you do. Thinking like an entrepreneur will help you in every aspect of your life. This book aims to help you to dispel the bad thinking habits we have all picked up along the way.

I wrote this book to tell you that being an entrepreneur is a state of mind. You do not have to start a business, you do not have to open a company; being an entrepreneur is more than that. Those things are merely the result of the entrepreneur's way of thinking. Being an entrepreneur means you greet every day confident that you are making your own decisions. You are an entrepreneur at home and at work.

It's Never About the Money demonstrates that, with a little bit of entrepreneurial thought, along with some hard work, you can be a success in whatever you do. This is how it was, this is how it is and this is how it always will be. In this book, I tell you what happened in my life, what I have done and what I have learnt. Throughout, I give you simple and accessible real-life lessons to help you to understand why and how.

The word 'entrepreneur' has been co-opted by the elite to make what they do sound extraordinary. They want people to believe this is something so foreign, so amazing, that only a very special few could ever do it. Being an entrepreneur is a way of life. More than anything an entrepreneur is a thinker and a doer. That is it: thinking and doing.

In this book, I will show you how attainable it all is. Far from special is the entrepreneur. You can do any of the things in this book. Ignore the fear we are all taught from birth. Don't listen to anyone unless they themselves have achieved.

There are no rules. The rule-makers – the elite – they are afraid; they want you to stay right where you are. They want you to continue as you were – to not even think about thinking. I am here to tell you there are no rules – not mine, not yours, not anyone's.

I am an entrepreneur. I want you to be an entrepreneur too in everything you do.

People will tell you that the definition of an entrepreneur is a person of extraordinary ideas. They are wrong. The people who came up with this definition are not in a position to do anything except observe and comment. They report what they think has happened. That is all they can do: report. They cannot explain why. They themselves have done nothing. An entrepreneur is first and foremost a human who thinks and acts without fear, without the fear other people have spent their lives learning.

When did I first know I was an entrepreneur? I probably didn't know when I sold my first bag of sticks aged eight. Maybe I didn't know when, as a 13-year-old, I left school and went to work in an assembly plant. I'm not sure I knew when I started work in British Leyland at the age of 17, or when I became a salesman at the age of 19. Odds are it was some time after that I began to realise – to realise that I was up for the adventure, that I relished it. Not only did I see opportunities, I saw beyond them.

I wanted life to happen; I wanted it to happen to me. The fear that others have, I've never had it. Why? Well, let me explain to you how I came about, how I have come to this.

More and more, as I got older, I felt that I was in a prison, a prison of my own making. I was both the guard and the prisoner. When I went to work for myself, or more accurately, when I became myself, I no longer had any thoughts like that.

This book is my explanation – my explanation of how I went about creating my future. How I stopped worrying and learned to love life, my life. My mother trusted me to think for myself; she always had my back, with very little interference. Although neither of us knew it at the time, this enabled me to do my own thing. There is nothing I have done that you could not do. There is nothing an entrepreneur does that you could not do.

I chose my own mind rather than everyone else's. I chose my own thoughts rather than everyone else's. I have been tapped on the shoulder by complete strangers and told that I would be OK. They have assured me that there were "tall people looking after me". And they left me alone thereafter, safe in the knowledge I was not alone. It would be a while before I woke up and understood what they meant. This is the story of how I recognised and opened my own mind.

I have always asked whether there was an easier way to do things. This would infuriate people no end. People are invested in the way things are. They love those strong walls they have erected around themselves. I did not set out to destroy those walls, but all through my life these 'experts' have put them in front of me. They have put them in my way. They have left me no choice but to go through them, over them or around them. Their lazy thinking, their second-hand ideas, rules, accepted practices, you name it, they have erected them right in my path. My path was always forward. My path was always a threat to them. A threat, for reasons I used not understand. Until one day I realised that people saw a reflection of their own lives in my choices, and that it was this that made them want to stop me. They tried to stop me accidentally or on purpose – or both. This negativity is the way of the world.

Repeat after me: "I am an entrepreneur".

Come with me. Listen to my story.

2: PAINTED STICKS

I was born in 1951. The birth of an entrepreneur is like anyone else's birth; don't let anyone tell you different.

In 1960, at the age of eight, I lived on a Corporation estate in South Dublin, Ireland. In my area, most people rented their house from the Corporation. Every few years, the Corporation would repaint and repair doors and gates. This was seen by people as an opportunity to perform minor renovations. One of the most popular renovations was to remove the huge kitchen press hung in each house. This press was removed to free up more space. Once down, the press proved awkward to store, and would often end up in the backyard until people could find a way to get rid of it. My parents did exactly this.

One day, my mother sent me out to chop the press into sticks to light the fire with. It occurred to me, as I watched the fire spark up quickly, that I might be able to sell these sticks. I went outside and set about chopping the press into manageable bundles of sticks, tying them together with strands of twine. My mother was happy to be rid of her press from the back garden.

I went door to door and, whether out of pity or need, people bought all the bundles from me in no time. I was delighted. Over the following few days, as I went to and from the shop for my mother, ladies asked me for more sticks. I heard others in the neighbourhood were asking after my sticks also. The consensus was that they lit very well. Usually, the local shop supplied the kindling but the ladies wanted my sticks.

One of my neighbours had a press in her back garden. She was fed up waiting for it to be collected. With my brother's help, I got the press back to our garden and chopped it into bundles of sticks. The presses were very heavily painted. It dawned on me, as I tackled the second press, that it was the paint that was causing them to burn so well. I said nothing. Off I went, same as before and the bundles of sticks were sold in no time. Even quicker perhaps, as people who had used them before bought extra. I made two shillings and sixpence (about 60c), which was great.

I started out early the next day looking for more wood, without much success. I found a door lying around, but that wasn't enough wood to do a round with. I spied some more doors and planks in the local dump. I puffed out my chest and went in to ask if could I have them. Initially, the security guard said "No", thinking I was going to use them for a bonfire. After I explained, he relented, allowing me only small batches of wood until such times as I had proved my innocence to him.

I brought the security guard back a bundle to show him I was on the level, as well as the newspaper to keep him happy. For the next while, I had as much wood as I needed. It was mostly unpainted so I asked the Corporation lads for some paint. They had been watching me, having a laugh, but they gave me the gloss paint I required. No harm in asking. There never is.

I painted planks, doors and floorboards. It did not have to be a neat job. I would leave them to dry for a couple of days, then break them up and off I would go on my rounds. I'd sell between 50 and 60 bundles each time and that made me a bit of money. Thinking about it all now, I never really got pocket money, the way my kids talk about it today. I don't remember getting a penny off my folks. I put the money I earned into a savings box.

I was to start work in the dairy soon. I have never not had a job, and I have never not had money. What is clear to me now is that I have always made my own money. I have never drawn the dole or social welfare or accepted any help from the State. I got into the habit of working early.

I was always a boring client for a bank manager. Avoiding debt as much as possible was always my aim. Someone once told me, "Stay out of the banks unless you're going to rob one". Sound advice.

Most of all, when I think back, I see from an early age that my instinct was to depend on myself, not someone else. I always wanted to get on with it. I liked to have a purpose. My mind had wandered around until it had figured out why people were so interested in my sticks. I figured out that the paint was making the difference. I was not any smarter than any other child. I simply allowed myself the time and space to figure it out.

Thinking and doing: the two things that have got me to where I am today.

The paint on the sticks was a slice of luck the first time. Identifying what my customers liked, and why they wanted it, changed stick-selling from a once-off into a mini-business.

Painted sticks. This was an invaluable lesson to learn so young. I have never forgotten it and I have used it throughout my life. Find out what your customer wants. Find out what your customer wants and give it to them.

3: CRITICISM IS CONFESSION

Here's a Confucian proverb:

He who knows not and knows not that he knows not, he is a fool –
shun him;
He who knows not and knows he knows not, he is simple – teach
him;
He who knows and knows not he knows, he is asleep – wake him;
He who knows and knows he knows, he is wise – follow him.

This ancient piece of wisdom exposed then what it still exposes today: life is full of wafflers. My uncle quoted this to me throughout my childhood. It was his favourite quote – if he had two quotes, I never heard the other one. He drummed it into me and I am thankful he did.

The only people who know are people who have done it.

Why did I become an entrepreneur?

I became an entrepreneur because I had to. My parents enabled me to grow up unhindered by negatives. Particularly my mother, she let me grow up unfettered by constant harrying, and she trusted me. More than that she let me know she trusted me, which was a great comfort.

My mother understood the importance of letting her kids think, helping us believe we could do it. Although she'd never learnt to read or write herself, she majored in one subject and that was allowing us to think for ourselves. She never articulated this idea to me and it is only now years later that I understand the gift. I now try to allow my own kids to think freely.

What about you? Do you feel hemmed in? Trapped? Do you feel like you are locked inside a system that has nothing to do with you? Maybe you do not like your job? Maybe you should think about leaving? Maybe you have been made redundant? Or more accurately, maybe your job has been made redundant?

Do you desire freedom? Entrepreneurs have a bohemian need for freedom. They have an attitude that does not accept boundary or structure. An accountant and an entrepreneur never see eye to eye. One is dedicated to structure, the other refuses to accept it.

My accountant once said to me, as he shook his head ruefully, "I am tired of looking at fools making money". Where should we start with that? If 'fools' are making money and he is not, then what does that make him?

The entrepreneur is always looking ahead, looking to the next step. People worry about the journey; the entrepreneur thinks about the destination.

Be mindful, even at this first stage, even as the first thoughts of becoming an entrepreneur appear, not to be dissuaded by the 'experts'. Everyone will try to put you off, except those who have succeeded.

Always remember it takes hard work, loads of hard work. Many people say they are trapped, lots of people say they want to change their lives, but they are not prepared to put in the work. They are not prepared to put in the thinking, to take the risk. They are mentally lazy.

Laziness, in whatever form, is the one thing that never sits well with the entrepreneur; there is no cure for it. Hard-worker, early-starter, willing to be free, to take chances, to live your life: these are the key attributes of an entrepreneur.

Remember that the entrepreneur is an independent soul. At the beginning, the entrepreneur is a fragile independent soul. You must do your best to avoid naysayers, they will drag you down. Your shoots of entrepreneurship could wither and die.

Don't listen when you hear:

o "Oh, you don't want to do that ..."

o "That will never work ..."

o "I know a guy who did that and ..."

o "You would be better off ..."

o "That was tried before ..."

All these things are said regularly, with authority, by the usual experts. If you must get advice, get it from someone who has been successful.

I was never able to understand why people felt the need to criticise my choices, when they had nothing to do with them. One day, it came to me: criticism is confession. If your family or friends are criticising you, they are confessing to you. Consciously or not, they are confessing to you their own inadequacies and fears. Do not heed them. Those who have achieved will not seek to bring you down.

So tread carefully. Do not seek the counsel of the well-meaning. Seek only your own counsel or the counsel of those who have succeeded in life.

THE JUNKYARD DOG AND THE POODLE

Inside each of us are two dogs, the junkyard dog and the poodle, the positive and the negative. Whichever one we feed grows and strengthens, it takes charge of our lives. As with anything in life, the one we practice, we perfect.

If we practice the negative one, we will be miserable and unhappy. Others around us will be miserable and unhappy. Look at the negative dog, it is angry and miserable; its only food is negativity. This causes anger, misery, anxiety and sorrow. The negative dog is not shy in asking for its food. Why feed it, why encourage it?

Look at the positive dog, it is a happy animal, contented and warm. When you are happy, all around you will be happy. Feed the positive dog. The more you practice feeding the positive dog with your actions and thoughts, the happier you, and those around you, will be.

By starving negative, positive appears and grows. Negative is the darkness; positive is the light. When you turn on the light, the darkness disappears.

Negativity is the mother of fear, anger, the need to control, lack of confidence, jealousy and hatred. All of these eat and devour their unsuspecting host. They cause unhappiness and low self-esteem. They always find others at fault when we all know in truth it is themselves. Negativity is practised by people from all walks of life; business people, teachers, bosses, mothers and fathers, friends and family. The negative junkyard dog will eat any negativity you throw at it, through thought, word or deed.

"The best way to find out if you can trust someone is to trust them." **Ernest Hemingway**

4: MILKING IT

Once my neighbours had burned every last stick in the area, I went into the dairy and got a job on a milk round; three to four hours a day before school, seven days a week. I rose every morning at 3am. My mother would get up with me, give me a cup of tea and a bite to eat, not too much as I got my breakfast when I got home. Two cod liver oil capsules kept my brain oiled.

I got this job – the kind of thing most lads were doing then – to earn a few bob, but it was never really for the money then or since. It was work, it was new and it was an adventure. Work got me where I wanted and it always fitted well with me. My parents, my mother in particular, were not keen on me working so young. But I earned 12 and a half shillings (about €5 now) a week; 10 to my mother, the rest for me, very useful. Having a job was a badge of honour. My parents let me know it was appreciated.

Besides the kudos, the best thing about having the milk round was the brown store-coat the milkmen wore. All the lads wanted one. The milkmen would give us an old one and we would bring it home and cut it shorter. Or more likely our mothers would cut them and sometimes put a hem on them. Once cut, they looked dreadful; we needed a belt to gather all the looseness from around the shoulders and the waist. The coats rode up because of the belts, and hence we called them 'bum-freezers'. They looked ridiculous really, but we never cared. We were heading to work; our bum-freezers let everyone know we were workingmen. After work, I would arrive home, relax on a chair for a bit, then off out to school.

It was an interesting job, a great education. Something that no longer happens these days, wherever you are from. The times were different. Think of a 12 year-old kid heading down the road at 3am to work: lugging crates, entering dark housing complexes, meeting locked-out drunks and homeless people. Was it right? Well, the words I use make it sound scarier than it was. I was toughened up nice and early; the choice was all mine and I never regretted it.

It really was different then; everyone felt safe, the postman, the milkman, anyone working felt secure. I could walk a couple of miles to play football with a friend, arrive home a little late without a bleep from anyone, save being told, "You are late for your dinner". Nowadays, kids don't venture out on their own much. They don't get to learn things like how to think, how to figure out how to get home, how to ask someone for directions or how to deal with bullies on their own.

Each day, our milk van would be left up at the depot for loading. Shaughnessy, who owned the milk round, arrived an hour later. By then, I would have the day's deliveries loaded. When I first started, we had a horse, Bob, and a cart. This was marvellous. Bob knew the route, when to stop and when to keep going. Unlike the truck, he never had any trouble starting. It was easy enough for me. Most people got the same thing Monday to Friday. Only at weekends did they get cream or Jersey milk. I would pick up empties and leave full ones. Simple and straightforward.

After four or five weeks, Shaughnessy informed me I had been loading the float incorrectly. He wanted me to remove the bottles from the top crate and hide them in the crates beneath. I was then to throw the empty crate onto the empty crate pile, before we passed the checker to sign us out. The few we left on top were to give the illusion of honesty. Every day, Shaughnessy was getting between six and eight unchecked bottles. Did the checker know what was going on? I am not sure. Thinking back, surely he must have known? He stood there, up on the bank, never getting too close.

A few weeks later, I got my second lesson. On the return to the dairy, I was told to crash two empty milk bottles against each other, then slightly remove one of the bottle tops off a fresh bottle and pour it over the broken bottles. This gave the illusion that two full bottles had broken. Roughly this gave the milkman, Shaughnessy, 62 bottles of milk a week to sell for himself. I never saw any of the money he received for it.

The two checkers, whom Shaughnessy had dubbed Sour Cream and Fresh Cream (sour being the slightly more stringent), never cottoned on. It was a great introduction to how most businesses worked back then. The whole experience made a deep impression on me. I always wondered how these guys could condone the stealing, or the graft. These things are what I call 'fat'.

This was the way things were done, so I said nothing. It stuck with me though, and while I was no saint, I never liked it.

5: LEAVING SCHOOL TO GET AN EDUCATION

When I left primary school in June 1964, aged 13, I was supposed to go onto secondary school; this was the law. I remember going down to enrol in a technical school. I can still see the big queue for the entrance exam. I didn't like the sight of it, so I left. I spent the morning elsewhere and told my mother that they only notified successful applicants.

My future brother-in-law got me a job in a factory, making and assembling window handles, metal shelving brackets, etc. My first job was to operate a large metal press punching brackets from steel sheets. After a while, I devised a new way that enabled me to punch continually, with only a nudge of the metal sheet in the right direction. It worked better, so long as I kept my foot on the pedal thus enabling it to run continually. By eliminating having to open and close the safeguard, it was quicker and safer as the guard stayed closed. Opening and closing the guard was the most dangerous action of the whole process.

Delighted with myself, I kept going at my new pace. I kept going until the next guy up the line from me complained I was going too fast. To avoid this, I used to take a break from my job and help him stack the brackets neatly, so he could process them more easily. Again, this guy I was helping complained to the union shop steward. The shop steward told me I was doing two jobs, to get back to my own job and operate the machine 'the normal way', as he put it. I could not really slow down; I had the machine running continually but safely. Once you find a better way, it is next to impossible to go back.

Eventually, the shop steward had our jobs switched. After a few days in my new position, I found an easier way to do things and again there was a problem. Our supervisor had been watching all this and was pleased; he insisted we continue with the new systems. He put me back in my original position to keep the push on. I could not understand what the problem was: surely a better production line was better for everyone? What about efficiency, speed and quality, two of which improved, one of which remained the same? I thought that an improvement being a good thing was a given. But, as we have all experienced in our lives, it is never a given.

The union guy's primary concern appeared to be keeping us under his control. The union rep had no real right to tell me what to do, or how to do it. I learnt fast the reality of the factory workers' experience: not allowed to think for ourselves or stand up for our sanity. Thinking for oneself did not go down well. I would often hear:

- o "Oh! Mister Independent."
- o "Why do you think you are different from the rest of us?"
- o "Why do you care?"
- o "Didn't realise you owned the place?"

This would be followed by some diatribe or abuse. No big deal, I suppose, as long as you keep your mind protected and are not cowed.

I decided then I would never be a follower. From then on, I would need to be convinced. People tend not to think for themselves; they just want to follow. Normally, they follow the loudest mouth.

A couple of years ago, a similar situation arose with a manager in my own business. I asked her why didn't she try x, y or z to ease the situation? She looked at me aghast and replied, "It is not my fault; I am only paid for thinking up to here", pointing at her neck. "Not my problem", she finished. She had resigned herself to being a lifelong follower.

For the followers out there, anybody who has any type of success is lucky:

- o "It landed into his lap."
- o "If she fell in mud, she would come up smelling of roses."
- o "Some people are born lucky."

This is the kind of thing followers talk about amongst themselves.

If you are involved in this type of thing, you are on the wrong train to everywhere, not just to being an entrepreneur. There is no point in a brush salesman complaining, "If only I sold vacuum cleaners". People still need brushes. Followers are everywhere; they consolidate their beliefs by mostly talking to each other.

The simple fact of the matter is, if you mix with non-doers or non-achievers, you will struggle. They will pull and drag you down. Mix with successful hard-workers and you give yourself the best chance to succeed. Believing you are entitled to it will not cut it.

Don't be a follower. Get involved. Be a player not a spectator.

The next couple of years were often uneasy for me. But I did have tall friends. Tall friends literally, so I was generally OK. Eventually, my mother heard British Leyland around the corner was looking for someone. Like all mothers, she wanted to be proud of where her son worked. In 1968, British Leyland was a big brand. It made Standard Triumph cars and Leyland Range Rovers. I was bright enough, with a head for figures, so I got a job in the parts department. All ordering was done manually. You were expected to learn things off by heart or consult one of the manuals. Microfilm was on the way in, but mostly we used memory or wrote things down.

I stayed in this comfortable job with sensible people for three years until I was 19. I bought a Ford Anglia 105E, one of about six cars on our road. I was making progress. Once someone got a job in British Leyland, they did not expect to go anywhere else. 'Set for life' was how it was put. In those days, people never appeared to change companies or ever really think about whether they were happy. This was especially true if they worked for a company like Leyland. People tended to stick to a job if it was deemed a 'good job' by their peers.

In 1970, by the age of 19, I had been promoted from £15 up to £19 a week. The promotion was worth more than just the money involved. I went from stacking and running orders around, to manning the phones and taking the orders from dealers around the country. The man I replaced had been transferred into another area. I got to know him well. It turned out that, when he had done my job, he had received £25 a week to my £19. I was a lot cheaper. I was paid for my age, not for my ability.

Everyone kept telling me I had a good job. Despite this, I felt penned in. I knew I could not stay where I was. I knew there was a natural ceiling. I was looking around for something that allowed me more scope for working independently.

I was observing and contemplating. Observation and contemplation: two skills everyone who wants to think like an entrepreneur needs to hone. I think, looking back, I was beginning to feel I was in that personal prison people often talk about. I was looking for the escape hatch. I wanted something more.

I remember getting the fright of my life seeing my foreman get his 25 years' service gold watch. As I stood there watching him receive his watch, I knew I needed to move. I needed to build myself a different future; nobody was going to create one for me.

Thinking of it now, I can see I was going nowhere. Thinking was not enough; I had to do something. I thought the guy to speak to was the foreman, the one with the 25-year watch. I mentioned to him that maybe I would try to get into sales.

He replied, "Ah no, Frank, sales is for better men than me or you".

Hello Confucius, this was a classic example of talking to the wrong fella! He stunned me, even hurt and frightened me. I thought for a moment, "God, is he right? Is there no way out? Am I a dreamer? Does he know better than me?". I got myself together, but it did take a few days before I saw him in a different light. Now I could see that he had included me in his low expectations. He had stayed in that same job until they retired him. Thinking about it now, he was only really talking about his own expectations. Criticism is confession.

HOW TO THINK LIKE AN ENTREPRENEUR

In Dublin, some years ago, I was walking down a main street towards a couple of phone boxes to make a call. I could see one box was empty and a queue of about five or six people at the other phone box. In front of me, a woman went for the empty phone box. She was told by the second person in the queue that the phone was not working, so she took her place at the back of the queue. Not fancying the wait, I headed for the empty phone box. The same person warned me. I ignored him and went into the empty box. I pushed all the buttons and some coins popped out. I heard the call tone. After successfully making my call, the guy with the big mouth gave me an earful, saying I should have let the next person use the phone first. The message, and there are several in this little story, is that I was a participant not an observer. I was a player, not a fan. I was the only one who believed the phone might work. I was optimistic. Above all, I was not afraid to be wrong in front of the big mouth and the rest of the people in the queue. I did not care what he thought. It was none of his business if I went into an empty phone box.

Some time ago, I was queuing at a buffet counter in a hotel for breakfast. The toaster was not working. Everyone was irritated. Nobody knew what to do. The employees shrugged and looked harried. The other guests, and the ever-present loud mouth, told everyone new in the queue, "The toaster is broken". I looked below the table, and saw that the toaster plug had come loose. I pushed the plug in. The toaster worked. Magic? No. Just thinking.

There are lots of similar examples from everyday life. Once you begin to see these scenarios, and approach them with clarity and self-assurance, things will get easier in work and in life. Do not be afraid to be wrong. You will be right seven times out of ten. Even in the smallest situation, the entrepreneur is at work.

6: LEARNING TO SELL

After much contemplation, in 1971 I decided I needed to become a salesman. Sales was the best job I could get without a formal education. It would lift my standing, it would elevate me and I could bypass the educational system. I might even get a company car. I was not content to be a follower for much longer. I did not want to spend my life blaming the obscure 'they' everyone talked about all the time. I did not want to blame anyone.

I applied for a job with Pitney Bowes, an American manufacturer and supplier of postal franking machines and photocopiers. After the interview, the interviewer rang me and told me the job had gone to someone known to the company. The interviewer insisted I had been the next choice.

Six months later, a junior salesman job came up in Pitney Bowes. I rang the interviewer back and I put it to him that, if I was second in line the last time, then I should be first in line now. He liked my approach and, despite the hundreds of applications, I started work the following week as a junior photocopier salesman. Photocopiers were then what computers are now: the future.

When I took the job, I went down to £15 a week from the £19 a week I had been earning in Leyland. Being a trainee, I earned no commission. I had to give all my leads to senior salesmen. I had to use my own car. In short, it was a risk.

I had a run-in with my dad, who thought it was madness. He hated the idea of people working on commission. I hesitated to tell him I was not even eligible for any commission. My Dad had worked for 43 years in Bewleys, an Irish catering company that produces tea and coffee. He was sceptical about anything different. We had a few extremely harsh words.

Luckily, I managed to get my mother on my side. I convinced her that the sales job was a risk worth taking. She was not happy, but she trusted me. After that, I felt able to go against my father. Without the support of my mother, I am not sure what I would have done. Sales commission jobs were new to my parents and they were reluctant at first to give me their blessing, but eventually my dad relented. I had always done my own thing. I probably would have taken the sales job anyway, with or without their blessing. But having my parents behind me made a huge difference and I drew great confidence from it. My mother even bought me my first suit to wish me good luck.

I started work as a salesman and I became very good at it. By that I mean I was a hard worker, like any other good salesman. Any salesman will tell you that 20 calls equal one sale. I never had the fear of rejection some had, as I figured out early that if someone says "No", then nothing spectacular happens. In fact, nothing happens except that you move onto the next call. So, the more time you get "No", the closer you are to a "Yes".

Then Pitney Bowes did away with the junior salesman position and I was offered a posting in either Glasgow or Edinburgh in Scotland.

Glasgow at the time was categorised as the world's most violent city. One night while I was doing my field training in Glasgow, a tall stranger, seeing me about to walk out of the hotel, approached me and warned me against going out locally. He told me my Irish accent would get me hurt. He showed me a picture on the hotel lobby wall with three slashed faces, otherwise known as 'Glasgow grins', with a warning underneath: 'BE CAREFUL WHERE YOU GO'.

So I chose Edinburgh. It was a strange situation: the head office was in Glasgow but I was expected to run my operation from my house and to store all the parts and machines there. After my two weeks training, I headed to Edinburgh with my demo machines, a map and a promise that, if I sold photocopiers to strangers, I would get money. If not, I would lose my job and I would not get any money. I never dwelt too long on these matters. It was all new to me and I saw it as a challenge.

Traditionally, all over the world, coffee shops are where salesmen meet other salesmen and swop leads. It was understood that you avoided salesmen in the same business as you; no leads there. After a few days checking out different places, a colleague in Glasgow gave me the name of a café he had frequented when he had worked in Edinburgh. Off I went. It proved worth the effort.

On my second or third visit, I introduced myself to a furniture salesman. He sat me down with his map and told me where to go. Or more accurately, he told me where everyone else went. The furniture salesman said something that has helped shape the way I have thought ever since. It has echoed through my whole life. He told me: "Go there, everybody goes there. Don't go there, nobody goes there".

This brought me up short. Why would I go where everybody else goes? But that is the perceived wisdom of life. This guy was a good guy, but he thought differently to me.

I had begun to think differently, although I was not aware of it yet. I decided I would go where no one else went. Off I went up the mountain to the old converted woollen and carpet mills above Edinburgh. Previously, the mills had been the big employers in the region. Every time I went up there, I was reminded that no matter how big or small you are, no matter how great it is at the time, you must always be changing and modernising. This failure to modernise, plus bad working practices, had brought the Scottish carpet industry to its knees. At one stage, the Scottish carpet industry had been the greatest on earth. But now the former woollen mills had been divided into manageable units and rented out to small businesses, the very businesses I had been advised not to visit.

The main advantage of going somewhere no one else went was that the office employees were not weary of seeing salesmen; in fact, often they were happy to chat for a while. My first move always has been to scout the premises, and to take down the companies' names from their nameplates. My next move is to knock on every door. Knocking on every door is how you keep sales high. Calls equal sales. They always have and they always will.

At the third door I knocked on, a young lady came out, asking me to wait while she copied some papers. While she photocopied, I asked her were there indeed 12 companies on the premises, always researching. I told her I was from Pitney Bowes and that we were promoting our copying range in the area in two days' time. She asked me, "Will you be showing your postal franking machines?".

"Of course", I replied and then asked, "Could we use the shared meeting room?".

"Sure, I will have it organised for you", she answered. These days, this use would be charged for, but not back then.

By the time I left her, she had given me the other 11 contact names I needed, one from each company. I asked her permission to tell people she would be looking at the franking machines. "No bother."

Obviously when I knocked on the doors, I worded it differently: "Joanne from Dowey Services and I have organised a demonstration, in the main meeting room, of our range of photocopiers and postal franking machines on Thursday. Would you be interested in attending the demonstrations?".

You must always be ready to grasp the opportunity when it presents itself. Through hard work, you will flush it out. I went on to sell three postal franking machines and three photocopiers at that demonstration.

In fact, instead of trying to sell the machines, I usually suggested leasing at £13 a month. Being asked to buy the photocopiers seemed to me to be more daunting. And there was a tax incentive to leasing, as it could be treated as a rental. I also used an ordinary Bic biro, rather than the fancy AT Cross pens used by most salesmen. Normally, I would not fill out the order form until afterwards. As soon as you started filling out forms and asking questions, people would get cold feet. Or worse still, they'd ask you to leave the form and to pick it up the next day. This was never a good idea. I asked them to sign on the dotted line; I would look after filling in the rest of the form later on.

It was not all sweetness and light, as any salesman can attest to. I was chased out of one office for being Irish. I was beginning a demonstration for some accountants when their boss walked in. He heard my accent and told me simply to get out "before I throw you out, you Irish bastard". That's the way it goes sometimes.

I became known as a good salesman and I ended up training the older fellows. For example, I taught them the 'assumed close': beginning the sale as if there are only a few minor details to work out, simply assuming that you are closing the deal. I would arrive into a demonstration asking the potential customer where they were thinking of putting the machine. I would look around and suggest, "Over there? Have you got a suitable table or would you like me to get one for you?". I would act as if the demonstration was a formality.

Some of the older guys learned and got better; others would snipe at me. It used to get to me sometimes. Nowadays, it would not bother me. The entrepreneur must learn to deal with naysayers. But at the beginning, the entrepreneur must strive to avoid them altogether, for nobody is more dangerous to the young entrepreneur.

It is important to remind ourselves what a salesman is exactly. A salesman is somebody who sells something to somebody, who does not know they need it, and otherwise would not have bought it. Brewery reps, coffee reps, reps of any kind are not salesmen. They are order collectors. Selling is a different thing altogether.

Salesmen needed to be sharp in those days. They were armed only with the Yellow Pages. Leads were as valuable as gold and were swapped between non-competing salesmen. Pitney Bowes was a really slick company with the sharpest of salesmen. It was a great place to learn. The competition fully respected us. We knew we had a reputation, and in the main, we upheld that reputation by going out and selling.

Pitney Bowes sent all new salesmen for training – two weeks in the Bonnington Hotel in Bloomsbury, London, all expenses paid. The fortnight was all about the science of selling. They took great care to recruit the right people and invested heavily in intense training. Once they invested in you, the conditions and terms were hard but understood by all.

In 1972, the contract read like this: "Your target is to sell three machines a month every month. You will receive a salary of £120 a week. Commission of £150 per unit sold. A fourth, and or any additional unit, is worth £200 per unit. Plus company car and expenses. If you fail to reach your monthly target, you will receive a letter of warning. If you fail to do so again the following month, you will receive a final warning. The third failure in a row will result in the termination of the contract".

Good money but tough terms. The warning process reset each time you sold the required three machines. I learnt that having no choice was the equivalent of an easy choice. There was nothing else we could do. The starkness of the options made everything clear.

I also learned there was a direct correlation between how hard you worked and how many machines you sold. During the weekly roundtable at the bar, mediocre salesmen would lament targets missed and the pressure. The successful salesmen would never hesitate to remind them that the reason they missed targets was they were not working hard enough.

"I saw your car outside the supermarket the other morning at 11.30. What were you doing in there? Why were you not out selling?".

"You're not doing your calls", we used to say to each other with pointed fingers. Calls equal sales.

7: THE OMEGA SYNDROME

My sales record in Edinburgh began to be recognised in the UK and Ireland. I came first in the monthly sales league table a couple of times over the next two years, and rarely left the top five.

I am not a superman. As I said, and this must be emphasised, it was achieved through calls and clear thinking. Learning and adjusting, acting and using what you have learnt. Always in the background and in the foreground is hard work. None of the thinking would have made a bit of difference without the hard work. Hard work is the magic.

In 1976, I was back in Dublin for the wedding of an old colleague. While there, I was approached by a representative of Hely Chambers, a subsidiary of the Smurfit group (Smurfit Kappa Group was Ireland's first home-grown multinational company and is now Europe's leading corrugated packaging company). The group had a problem. Xerox had held a monopoly in the plain-paper copier market until the Federal Trade Commission intervened in 1975, after which Xerox was forced to forfeit patent protection and had to license competitors. Up until then everybody else had used one treated paper or another. In Scotland, I had sold zinc oxide copying machines. Once the Xerox patents were finished, other brands like Canon, Olympia and Mitsubishi entered the plain paper copier market.

Hely Chambers had purchased 200 Olympia Omega plain paper copier machines, to compete with the market dominators Xerox. They had hired ex-Xerox salesmen and had aggressively targeted the Xerox plain paper market in Ireland. Hely Chambers soon discovered the German Omegas did not work in the offices they were placed and often went on fire. The plan rapidly became a complete disaster and everyone connected got the sack: salesmen, managers, everyone. This was a massive embarrassment to all involved. Everyone felt the shame, and nearly 200 Omegas lay untouched for seven months.

I was invited to the warehouse to have a look at the machines. Hely Chambers did not know me from Adam. But they had heard from an old colleague that I could sell photocopiers. I was dealing with people in senior management; I was 25. They wanted to know what I thought; they wanted my advice. "Can they be sold or can't they?" was really all they wanted to know.

They showed me the Omega in action. It was quite slow and needed to be kept switched on all day. It had a couple of other inadequacies the Xerox machines did not have. I kept my counsel and said I needed to think. Clear eyes, clear thoughts. Relaxing and allowing yourself time and space to think.

"Why were they selling this machine as a Xerox replacement when it was clearly not?", I thought. The salesmen had targeted customers they knew used Xerox, and sold them the Omega. The Omega was unable to handle the same volume level as the Xerox machines and often would set the paper on fire. The salesmen were all ex-Xerox, so they had done what they knew.

People go on all the time about turning a negative into a positive. They never explain what they mean. Well, this is one example. The weakness of the Omega was its inability to deal with high volume. So the answer lay in its weakness. The Omega could not handle high volume. Answer: sell it as a low-volume machine to offices that only needed a low-volume-copier!

I went back to Hely Chambers for a second meeting. Hely Chambers was already selling zinc oxide machines. They were low volume and very expensive. In addition, the expensive treated paper they used was not nearly as attractive as the plain paper. You could save money with the plain paper Omega and get rid of the pungent zinc oxide machine. Customers would be happy.

I saw that by replacing the zinc oxide machines with the Omegas, we could shift them. This solution was right there in front of everyone. They had not thought about it properly, and hence had not seen it. The Omega was priced at £1,800. I suggested increasing the price to £2,300, with £200 of the extra £500 being mine. They were delighted and, despite not knowing my strategy, they agreed to the deal.

I left my job in Scotland and went back to Ireland. I began my job with Hely Chambers by going to see the service department. They told me the Omegas were a complete nightmare. I explained I thought it was more a matter of them being used in the wrong volume offices. They agreed with relief.

I asked them about the zinc oxide machines. "Yeah, we sell loads of those."

I replied, "Well, next time someone with a zinc oxide machine rings up about a service or a problem, could you explain that, for no extra cost, they can have the Omega plain paper machine?". I taught the service people how to sell the idea and gave them £20 of my own money for each lead.

Next I went and found who the biggest zinc oxide paper purchasers were. I knew I could save these people money as well.

I got rid of all the Omegas in two years.

This was not a particularly complicated solution. It was the reverse; it was a simple solution. The cliché is correct: the simplest solution is the most difficult to see, at first anyway. Believing there is a solution is always the first step.

I knew through my own experience that you can turn a negative into a positive. I understood this was not a myth, because I had done it myself. I allowed myself time and space to think, to let the various aspects of the problem percolate through my head.

People are invested in something being impossible because they cannot do it, or more accurately, they are afraid to try. They are worried they will be shown up. They are more worried they will be shown up than they are about finding a solution. This makes them reluctant to believe anyone can do it.

Relax, believe, think and understand, the solution will come.

IT'S BROKEN

Here is a story. It is an everyday story, only relevant because of how normal it is and how often it happens. It's about the fax that was not broken.

I had an assistant called Deborah. She worked in the office beside mine. One day, I told her I needed to send a fax. She answered, "The fax is broken". This was the early 1990s and a broken fax was a serious matter. I accepted this for about 20 seconds before asking, "What's wrong with it?". She answered, "It is broken". I asked again, "I know, but what is wrong with it?". She answered, "Obviously, it is not working". My interest piqued, I went into her office. I asked, "Why is it not working?". She answered, "Jenny, from administration, was trying to use it yesterday evening and she told me it was broken". I asked again, "So what is wrong with it?". She answered, "I presume you cannot send faxes". I asked, "OK, can you receive faxes?". She answered, "Well, if you can't do one, you can't do the other". I replied, "Not necessarily true. Sometimes you can receive and not send". She retorted, "Well, she just told me it was not working".

I took a look at the fax. The cover seemed to be askew so I pressed down on it. It clicked into place, and the fax made a little whirring noise. Deborah's eyes opened wide, but she said nothing.

I sent my fax and it seemed to work.

But now Deborah wanted to protect her esteem, so she dug in. She predicted, "He probably won't get it". I asked, "Why won't he?". She reaffirmed, "Because it is broken". I asked again, "Who said it was broken?". She replied, "Well, the engineer is on his way. I rang him and, even though he was on his way somewhere else, I got him to turn back because it was so urgent. He will be here soon".

I asked Deborah to ring the engineer and tell him it was a false alarm. Unless I had examined the fax, the engineer would have come, claimed to have found something wrong with the machine, and charged us. Forevermore, the record would have shown that on that date the fax machine was broken.

Meanwhile, I'd rung the recipient, confirmed receipt of the fax and asked him to send me back a test fax, with a squiggle on it to ensure everything was working the other way. He did and it was.

Deborah was a good employee and afterwards, when she realised what had happened, she learnt from it. It is important to remember Deborah was not aware she was doing anything wrong. She thought she was doing the right thing by ringing the engineer.

I had asked the same question eight times but could not get past the self-esteem barrier. This happens on a daily basis in most organisations one way or another. People will do almost anything to protect their self-esteem. It is your job to persist and challenge until you get the response you need.

People are simply waiting for things to go wrong. They believe instantly and easily that something is broken or out of stock, because it lives down to their expectations. People expect these self-erected barriers and then cease all forward movement. Having invested themselves, they become committed to the story, and hence they are reluctant to help solve the problem. These mis-identified problems allow people to do nothing, and give them permission not to think any further.

The entrepreneur must identify, locate and fix all problems, daily, weekly and monthly. They can take any form. Sometimes they are an imagined piece of broken equipment. Sometimes they are decades-old unwritten rules that everybody is following. Whatever they are, they need to be swept away.

8: THE SALLINS TRAIN ROBBERY

I enjoyed the Omega success and I was on to the next thing. My friend Vincent had been asked to a secret bank meeting in the HQ of AIB, one of Ireland's largest banks. All he'd been told was that it was a paper-handling problem. All very intriguing. Vincent did not fancy going on his own. So off we went together.

We were shown into AIB HQ; into a board meeting with 17 guys in the room. It was the biggest board meeting I was ever at; us in our 20s, the rest roughly in their 90s. Before we were told anything we swore our secrecy on the Bible, excited and unaware of what was to come.

A train carrying soiled, worn bank notes to the Central Bank for destruction had been robbed earlier that week. £200,000 had been taken. It became known as The Sallins Train Robbery. The cash was untraceable, in non-sequential notes. The bank needed us to come up with a paper-handling solution that would prevent this type of robbery from happening again. They wanted to avoid paying for soldiers on the trains. They also required a solution quickly.

I suggested guillotining the notes and putting each half on a separate train. The bank was interested, but dismissed the idea, due to problems in matching the notes and the anticipated refusal of the Central Bank to accept notes cut in half.

We left the meeting being reminded we were still under oath. Back at the office, I saw someone using a Wiro Bind, a machine that binds reports with wire, such as you would see on a calendar. This gave me an idea.

Using a Wiro Bind, I practised with some photocopied pound notes. The next week, Vincent and I went back to the bank to demonstrate what we could do with photocopied notes and a Wiro Bind.

This time, only seven people met us. Although we were told off for photocopying money, the bank liked the Wiro Bind idea. They wanted it mechanised and for it to punch holes in the shape of the diamonds on playing cards. One other stipulation: the punch had to avoid the numbers on the notes and the anti-counterfeit silver metal strip. No problem, we thought.

Our CEO gave us the go-ahead to speak to Wiro Bind about the project. Wiro Bind was interested. After some back and forth, we came up with a mechanised machine that punched holes in the notes. These machines cost £25,000 each; they also needed constant maintenance. We sold quite a few of them. Between maintenance and sales, Smurfit came out of it well. For a few years at least, there were no more train robberies. We were responsible for the invention of the machine that stopped them.

Believing that there is a solution is the first step. Once you have unfettered your mind, the solution will come. Allow the answer in. Don't listen to people who tell you it cannot be done.

If you want something, you have to go get it. If you want light, you need to flick a switch. If you want a machine that binds bank notes into a wire holder, so people won't rob a train, you need to go and get one. What? There is no such thing? Then you need to go and invent one. Right? Right.

THE BUSINESS BOAT

Generally, a business has a Sales department, an Administration or Finance department and a Service department. Each part of the business represents a different part of the 'Business Boat'.

In a lot of businesses, these departments don't have a good relationship. Normally service and sales do not get on. And of course, the people in admin simply turn on the heating, relax into their desks and chill out. This leads to departments being isolated, and often leads to the death of the company. This separation used to be more understandable when we knew less about how a business functions. Now we know differently.

The business boat helps us to see clearly; if there is a problem in Service, then the Sales guy cannot close his door to the problem. If there is a problem in one section of the boat, that is a problem for everyone. Irrespective of where the boat has sprung the leak, everyone will drown if the leak is not addressed. Everyone should be willing to participate in the solution to the problem. Everyone has an input.

Departments and titles separate people, and individualise responsibility. The separation is an illusion; it only exists for ease of organisation. It is a hindrance when it comes to people acting in unison. Teach your employees that everyone is in it together. Job titles enable people to believe they are not responsible for things not directly referenced in their job title. Job titles do more harm than good. All through my life I have witnessed this.

All employees should understand what the other sections do. Everyone should be prepared to bail out the other departments. Everyone needs to understand they are all in the same boat. The team, or the group, is an essential tenet of business. Employees often work harder simply because they do not want to let anyone down. The business boat demonstrates to your employees how you are all in it together.

9: PETTICOAT LANE

Later in 1976, my boss in Hely Chambers sent for me again. He told me, "We have a problem and you are the man for the problem".

Smurfit had been on an acquisitions drive. They had acquired a group of companies. Inside Smurfit, these companies made up the stationery group. This man Costello was the new CEO of the stationery group.

"Confidentially", Costello said twice, "confidentially, we are looking to tidy up these companies and then close them down. We are meeting with a lot of resistance from the managing directors. They are all in the same group and are very tightly knit".

He continued, "Henry Jackson, a stationery company, is holding a huge amount of stock, but doesn't know how much. I need somebody to get involved; to do something about all the stock".

Costello wanted me to go into this stationery company, Henry Jackson, to find out how much stock they had, and sell it at a profit. I would probably encounter some problems from senior management, but I was to get it done irrespective.

"No one in their right mind would take that job", I said.

"I know", he said, "that's why I am asking you".

I told Costello I needed a letter outlining how I was to be given full access, and explaining how I reported directly to him only. I got two copies of this letter and used it like a licence. Without it, I would not have been allowed in the door.

Some of the stock had been sitting around for 14 or 15 years. Much of the older stock consisted of things like sharpeners and erasers.

One positive, which struck me immediately, was that at least it would be cheap. Nobody else seemed to have thought about this. Everyone was keen to protect their own fiefdom, no matter how small. Maybe the company could have been saved if people had acted earlier, although that was never said. Nobody seemed to see it, despite the fact it was right in front of their eyes. It was right in front of their eyes, but behind their self-esteem.

It was a stationery company with lots of clients. Had the people there ever thought to offer the stock to their existing customers at a knockdown price? This is a classic example of a company that failed to grasp the tenets of the Business Boat. A lot of people in Henry Jackson believed all they needed to do was to protect themselves; they believed the water would never reach them.

On my first day at Henry Jackson, the MD met me and warned me that a 'young pup' like me was not going to show him up. He alluded to dark forces at work in the stationery group. It was always the group, never the company. The group felt there was safety in numbers. Initially, the MD refused to give me a pass or an office, so I showed him my letter. He relented slightly and I got an office.

Foolishly, on my first day, I left my belongings in the office and they were stolen. I was so unpopular it was hard to know who not to suspect. You live and you learn. I was only 26 and the boss was in his mid-50s. I often forgot this, how it could make someone feel. The gloves were off; remember I was the hired gun going over his head. My intention had been to work with him, but he had reacted badly. The employees also seemed to have been warned, as they kept their distance.

I went and had a look at the stock. Felt markers drying out, rusting pins, pencils of all makes and sizes. Who knew there were so many types of pins? Overall, the place was a mess.

I went back to the CEO and told him I was having problems. He told me to grow up and stop crying.

The next bright idea I had was expensive. Bribe the staff. My own bonus system, like I had used in Hely Chambers.

The lady who ran the stores was the first one I approached. She had 25 years' experience and was the only one with the wherewithal to understand the stock. I bowed down to her, told her how great she was, and that she was the linchpin of the company. She was paid poorly for someone with such an important job; praise seemed to be a poor substitute. I offered her some money to help me. She was glad of the money and the attention, pleased someone had noticed her ability and knowledge. I asked her for a full inventory and, despite the amount of work it entailed, she dived straight in. All of this went on without the knowledge of the MD.

One of the other MDs in the group, on hearing I was going to try and get rid of the old stock, scoffed at me in the corridor one day and, in between snorts of derision, he suggested, "Why don't you go over to Petticoat Lane? They buy sh##e there".

Laughing in my face, he thought he was hilarious, that he had scored one for the group. This proved to be the second time in my life I had been told the truth except in reverse. By sarcastically telling me to go to Petticoat Lane, he had told me exactly where to go.

Off I went to London. I was looking for guys who had cash for a good quick bargain. It had to be a great deal, something the other guys in the market did not have.

Petticoat Lane was, and is, a huge market for absolutely anything and everything in London. I went down to have a look, to smell, feel and observe the business; learn what was going on. As I suspected, these traders were sharp and fast – hard men. I spent two days walking around soaking it all in. It seemed to operate along barely legal lines. Once money had changed hands, there was no going back, no matter what. There was no after-sales service department to call if you had a problem in Petticoat Lane.

But, after a couple of days walking around, I was convinced it was the right place. The bigger traders were hard to find and did not like my suit or, especially, my accent. Who was I to them? Nobody.

I was looking to sell the stock in bulk and extremely cheaply. I had set myself up in the London Tara Hotel near Kensington. I learned all the relevant businesses from the Yellow Pages. The Yellow Pages did not give me the inside track though. This assignment was about wits, quick thinking and no rules. It was hard ball all the way along – even getting to speak to someone, anyone, took a few days.

Eventually, I was directed to some warehouses by a newspaper seller who had waited for me to buy a newspaper, before answering my query.

"Have you any idea how many people ask me for directions every day? I sell newspapers."

So I had bought a newspaper, laughing.

He was one of them. The newspaper seller told me what I needed to know and, more importantly, where I needed to go. Without him, I might still be there.

After four or five calls, and being chased out of more than one warehouse for being Irish (this was not long after the IRA had blown up pubs in Birmingham and Guildford), I met a guy who showed some interest. I was told to wait while he fielded enquiries on the phone for the guts of an hour. Meanwhile I pretended to be interested in his stock, never hurried him. I stayed cool, pondered, not wanting to be told to come back another time. He was a busy, busy man. When the phone at last took a break, he beckoned me over. I stood in front of him for a minute.

"So what is your story? You have not waited here for my benefit. Must be a good one in this for you."

"A good deal is one with good profits to both sides", I replied.

He paused, looked up at me again and asked me to repeat what I had just said. I did and he wrote it down.

Traders like him usually bought fire-damaged stock from insurance companies, and sold it from stalls at markets like Petticoat Lane. You could buy a nice shirt there, only to bring it home and find that it was missing a sleeve. Returning it was not an option; the guarantee ceased when their fingertips touched your cash. The name Petticoat Lane supposedly came from the story that "they would steal your petticoat at one end of the market and sell it back to you at the other".

The trader opened my doctor's briefcase and examined the markers and pencil sharpeners. Usually the buyer would have looked for brand names, to ensure some semblance of quality, but in those days most markers and sharpeners did not have recognisable brand names.

We then started to talk about price; always a good sign.

He tested the markers and thankfully they worked. I have often wondered what would have happened if they had been dry. I was biting my lip while he did his tests. His next question blew me away, "How much have you got?".

I had around £150,000 worth of markers. That price allowed him to double his money and move them fast. I told him, "I think you are the type of guy who writes down a wise message when he hears it. With my price, you would double your money, but you would have to take all of them. £150,000". I was hardly breathing.

Taking a marker, he made a phone call to another dealer friend. He turned and asked me where the markers were from.

"Italy". I showed him the country of origin on the side of the marker.

According to his partner on the other end of the telephone line, Italy made the best markers. Originally, my guy had indicated he needed to speak with three other partners. But the first partner he rang told him not to bother calling anybody else; the two of them could handle it.

His phone partner also wanted the sharpeners, telling us he had a contact in London schools. "Better price there than in the market", he quipped. I also managed to get them to take the pencils for £30,000. They had to ring the schools contact. He confirmed his interest saying the schools would take all the sharpeners, erasers and pencils.

We did the deal, getting letters of credit from the dealer's bank and shipped the lot.

Next up were the rubber bands, small paper punches, more pencils, pins of all sizes, staplers, lever arch files and on and on. I thought to myself that night in the hotel: "What type of business could use these things in bulk?".

I pondered and I contemplated. Answer: banks and government departments. I contacted a range of both the next day by phone, arranging for them to be sent samples from Dublin to peruse. Of course I always explained and emphasised that they could save a fortune. As far as I know, to this day, banks use pins instead of staples on their paper files. The banks and the insurance companies took the pins and almost everything else.

After three weeks, great progress had been made in shifting the stock mountain in Henry Jackson. I need to point out here, once again, inside the negative lay the positive. The stock was very old and often was not much use. This was the weakness as well as the strength; because of this, it was very cheap. I understood this, and knew that I had to sell it in bulk but it would be very cheap.

I arrived back one morning and there was a great buzz about the place with the goods being shipped over to the UK. Last in as per usual was the MD. He ignored me. The employees had misinterpreted the news. They had been told many times that, if they shifted the stock, the business would stay alive. But the Business Boat had shipped a lot of water, there were too many leaks. I moved some more stock on the Irish market. None of this made any difference as the place was fated to close. One of the buyers of a huge consignment of rubber bands was already a customer of Henry Jackson. This customer's office was only 500 yards down the road.

Two months after my trip to London, with final sales from the old stock touching £850,000 and my project complete, Henry Jackson closed. The boat sank. The solution was not rocket science, the solution was right in front of them, but they would have had to have worked for it and gone out on a limb. None of them wanted to work together. It was always someone else's problem.

I was back to where I had started. I was back working for Hely Chambers. Although I never felt like I was really working for them, I always felt apart. I felt at this stage that I was working for myself. I had had a few successes. I was reminded that thinking differently sets you apart. I understood I was different but I did not really analyse why.

Over the years I missed having people to celebrate with; however, I did not miss it enough to stop me moving forward. This goes to the core of being an entrepreneur. It is often a lonely road. Once you begin proving people wrong and punching through their self-esteem, you can expect to be isolated until you find your own people. Entrepreneurs have to work a lot on their own. If their thoughts are contaminated, they lose their effectiveness.

10: CLEANING UP

More and more, I felt confined by working for someone else. By 1978, I was getting tired of office equipment, of having to prove myself anew every month. I also wanted my independence. Essentially, I could not stand having anyone in charge of me. This desire to be my own boss drove me.

I was offered a job in Dublin with a UK building services company called Enright. The first thing that struck me was that in building services everything is paid monthly; it is really a rental business. Enright provided cleaning and maintenance to companies and government departments that outsourced, or as they called it then, contracted out. The offer was very good basic money. I was interviewed by the Irish MD and the head salesman. I was distinctly underwhelmed by both of them, but I told them I would consider it.

This concept of contracting out building services – cleaning or maintenance, for example – was quite new in Ireland. Being offered the job was the first time building services had come to my attention. I looked further into the young industry and felt good about it. I sensed it was ready for expansion. I had an investor who was keen to invest in something that involved rental or monthly payments – anything with a regular income.

The interview had sparked my interest. I did more research and discovered the building service sector was largely underdeveloped. I believed the time was right to make a move into it. I wanted more action. I told my investor about the idea and he liked it. We agreed to instigate a plan. Neither of us knew anything about building services. That was our first task, to learn about the business. I suppose we should have been afraid but it never really occurred to us.

I took the job with Enright to do some on-the-job research for opening our own place. Of course, they did not know that – and I did not tell them. My plan was to work for six months and learn as much as possible.

The business was defined by the management of people. The people were the product. Dealing with people is both very demanding and very rewarding. They bring their problems to you and, whether you like it or not, the onus is on you to find a solution. There is nothing more enjoyable. Learning about people and managing them has been the most enjoyable and fulfilling experience of my life.

I noticed British Home Stores, a large British department store, was moving onto O'Connell Street, Dublin's main thoroughfare. I went down there eight or nine times to have a look and try to talk to someone – and eventually I did. They allowed me to tender and we won the contract. It was £52,000 a year. It was the biggest contract Enright Services had won in a while – even the MD was impressed.

The salesman from the interview asked me, "Do you want to pool our sales?".

I said "No". This was not the behaviour I expected from him, a fellow salesman.

The owner also began to begrudge and delay paying me my commissions. He felt I had not earned them, that it was all down to luck. Whether it was down to luck or not seemed to me irrelevant. A deal is a deal. This released me from the guilt I was feeling about leaving sooner rather than later.

I set about learning as much as I could. Most of it was relatively straightforward, apart from the pricing. Pricing was the key to every tender, to every contract, to everything. If a job was not priced correctly, it would result in future problems when managing the contract.

I took a second job working with Enright in St Vincent's Hospital. Hospitals have the most diverse costing jobs, so I felt I would benefit. I worked in a different section every two nights. This was a great way to learn, although it did alert the MD to my intentions. So he called me in.

"Why are you working nights in the hospital?"

"To learn how to price."

"Yeah, but why are you doing it?"

"To learn how to price."

"Nobody has ever done that before."

"I am worried that, if I price a job incorrectly, we will lose a lot of money."

The MD did not buy it. I felt I might be about to get the boot.

Shortly after my run in with the MD, I was chatting with the main service contracts manager, McLaughlin, who was complaining about the MD. I asked him, "Have you ever thought about going out on your own?".

"I've thought about it loads of times", he answered.

"Have you? Well, I am not going to be working here forever. I am going to go out on my own eventually. If you made a move, that would force my hand. I would make a deal with you", I told him outright.

I was about 27 at this stage. McLaughlin thought about it the rest of the week, then went to the MD. I stood my ground. I told the MD, "I've never claimed I would stay forever. Of course, I will leave eventually".

I explained the conversation had been born out of what McLaughlin had said. "I merely asked him not to leave without me."

The MD left the matter at that. McLaughlin was far too valuable for him to force the issue, since he ran the entire service team. The MD asked me what my real intentions were. I told him, "I will stay here until I decide to go and work for myself, somewhere else".

I managed to stay there another two months, then handed in my notice. The investor put up £7,000, and the bank matched it. We set up Professional Contract Services with no contracts.

Our first contract was for David Brown Tractors. We struggled at the beginning to get the managers we wanted, as the business had a bit of a stigma. I remember telling the Smurfit guys what I was going to do. They all fell around laughing, even the bad salesmen. They wanted to distance themselves from it. It was not Ferraris or banks or airlines. The leaving card they gave me was littered with warnings about how I had made a mistake, "You will regret it" and, of course, "You are crazy".

I have to say their messages pulled me up short, made me look again at my decision. It was contract services, at least at the beginning. No matter, I thought it was underdeveloped and I felt good about it. This may be the crux of the matter. They thought they saw one thing, while I saw another. We were both looking at the same thing.

When we came along in 1978, the building services sector was transitioning from internal cleaning departments to outsourced services. The problems we encountered helped me to understand people more, and also I think, to run the business better.

In building services, there were two particular issues we struggled with at first. The first problem was a plague of broken vacuum cleaners; the second was supplies running out before the end of every month. Both issues were used as an excuse by employees for poor performance. Both issues resulted in buildings and offices not being sufficiently serviced – and clients complaining.

There was a general perception in the industry as a whole that nothing could be done about either of these problems; this was the way things were. Both problems were people problems. Both were unnecessary, but they are indicative of the type of issues faced by business all over the world.

As we began to expand in Ireland, we copied a lot of the basic practices and internal structures of other building service companies. This had advantages but also disadvantages. We were able to put the company together very quickly. However, we also inherited the faults and weaknesses that went along with these structures and systems.

Our employees worked in the clients' buildings rather than in ours, so there was an unusual closeness between our employees and our clients. Whenever a complaint was made, the client naturally would believe everything they were told by the employee. This typically led to the blame being left at the illusory door of 'the company'. Not even 'head office', merely 'the company'. Teaching your employees that they are this illusory entity is difficult. Teaching your employees that they are 'the company' is a challenge. Teaching your employees that they are the company, that one thing impacts us all, this is never-ending. Don't take it on, if you are not up for it. I began to realise that the employees thought they were separate and immune to the problems of the business. At the start, a lot of the employees felt they were not even in the same boat as each other; they felt some employees had one boat, management had another and so on.

The employees would tell the client that the reason the job was not done was because the vacuum cleaner was broken or they were out of supplies. These were perfect problems as they were out of the employee's control and, in their eyes, got them off the hook. They protected their self-esteem. So we were getting complaints from clients regarding the standard of cleaning. The complainant would mention how the company had left the cleaners without supplies or the vacuums were broken and nobody had come to fix them. Once I began to study and analyse the complaints, a clearer picture started to emerge.

I knew I had to deal with it properly and thoroughly as it was impacting things across the business. These issues were bringing in a general air of malaise, an acceptance of failure or inadequacy. We were all in the same boat. Every problem in your business is your problem.

During a brainstorming meeting, I asked 15 managers, "How many people have had a vacuum cleaner break at home in the last month?". Nobody answered.

"Two months?" Nobody.

"Six months?" Nobody.

There was no answer up to a year. I got two things out of this.

First, the employees were not looking after the vacuum cleaners as they would their own. Second, I began to suspect that maybe the vacuum cleaners were not broken at all. The bigger contracts, the bigger jobs, had almost no issues like this. The bigger jobs had managers constantly supervising. Bigger clients tended not to have a personal relationship with our employees. Although the vacuum cleaners on the bigger jobs were used more, they were reported broken much less often.

After much investigation, I came to the conclusion that both these problems were, in the main, imaginary. Most of the time, both these things were excuses. Of course, when the client was ever given either of these excuses, they would never check. They took the employees' word for it. Why wouldn't they? Most of the buildings on the smaller jobs were cleaned every day, so even if the supplies were a day late, it should not have resulted in an instantly noticeable problem. Cleaning is mostly just water, soap and elbow grease. This helped me understand this was not merely a supplies problem; employees were using the supplies as an obstacle to their work. Simply put, they would not wipe a table if there was no polish.

To solve the vacuum cleaner issue, we began checking up on all these broken machines. Generally, we found they were working fine. The conversation then typically went like this. It was all about protecting self-esteem.

"I thought the vacuum cleaner was broken?"

"Jim must have come and fixed it."

"No, he didn't fix it", I would reply.

"He must have fixed it because it was broken yesterday", the employee would retort.

We would then plug it into the socket and it would work. I could hear echoes of the broken fax machine. We would continue on and look at the next broken one, again same thing.

"It must have been the socket was on the blink."

"So who told you it was broken?"

"Betty told me."

We knew we were never going to win this war. Getting the employees to admit they were in the wrong was a pointless task.

Why did we not sack them? They only acted like most people act. It was much better to change the system. All reports of broken vacuum cleaners were to be considered false, unless confirmed by a manager. If the vacuum cleaners were genuinely broken, we had an easy solution because we used the top of the range Nilfisk. It had detachable parts and our managers had replacements parts in their car. If there was something wrong with the vacuum cleaner, the onus was on the manager to replace the broken part, the broken lead or the broken motor. This was easily and quickly done.

We had a meeting where we explained what was going on. We told our employees we did not believe that the broken vacuum cleaner epidemic was real. We insisted any incidents of broken machinery be checked and dealt with immediately by a supervisor or a manager. No exceptions. We explained to our managers that employees were making up stories about their vacuum cleaners. We encouraged them to ensure people were looking after their vacuum cleaners correctly. We transferred the responsibility for maintenance to the area managers. The area managers then got the supervisors involved. The supervisor had the parts and knew their boss was following up on what was going on. They became more rigorous in checking up on what people told them.

In essence, people were making it up; this endangered their own jobs and damaged their company. This was a people problem, though not an unusual one. People act against their own interests all the time. This particular problem highlighted the danger of not observing closely what is going on in your own business. Check everything regularly, be familiar with what is going on. It also was the beginning of the idea for the Business Boat. I could not understand why the employees were sabotaging their own company.

The next issue was the supplies. We looked at the facts. The managers running out of supplies were having to order top-ups before the month was out. To solve this problem, we came up with a specific day for each manager to have their supplies delivered. John's supplies would be delivered on the second of the month. If this date was a Saturday or Sunday, then his supplies would be delivered the following Monday. Everybody knew when the supplies were expected. This answered the question of when they got delivered. We measured cleaning products per head per month. We had every manager come up with job-specific monthly orders. Every job was to get the same order irrespective of what month it was. We also stopped giving them a budget to spend on supplies; instead we asked how much supplies were needed. By focussing on what supplies were needed rather than giving them a financial budget, we saved £62,000 in the first year. Astonishing.

Each and every contact was set up like an individual business. Every contract had to make money on its own.

When we moved to England, we discovered it was the norm for managers to come into head office on one Friday every month and do their monthly order. They would lose a day of productivity. We changed that. We instigated the systems we had in place in Ireland; one clear unchanging monthly order. Each contract had to stand alone.

We learnt a lot from this. We learnt not to take anyone's word for anything. This is a hard lesson but a necessary one. Your employees will be constantly on the lookout for reasons to avoid doing what they are supposed to be doing. It is too easy to say they were lying. What happened, what continues to happen all over the world to this day, was that if the vacuum did not work immediately, it was considered broken. Unless you know something yourself, you do not know it. This was the lesson we taught our managers time after time. Hearsay is nothing. Double check.

When people see themselves as separate to the company, then they have no problem damaging the company, or running it down. This is a difficult lesson to swallow, but one that every entrepreneur must remember. Teach your employees and get them to understand they are the business. Explain to them the analogy of the Business Boat, show them how everyone depends on one another in business.

A business does not make money; people make money. You cannot do it without them. This is a revelation for many people, but it is the people in the business who make the money.

The lesson learnt from the supplies issue was that systems must be put in place and adhered to. For systems to work, checks must be made on top of checks on up the line. We worked on the basis that if we had three or more employees in any location, we needed to pay one of them to act in a supervisory capacity. The only reason anyone ever ran out of supplies was if they were using more than they needed, or someone was stealing, or the monthly order was incorrect. Eliminate whatever variables you can.

People are the main variable; using process and systems can cut down on error and inefficiency.

Also beware of managers or anybody else telling you, "She told me …" or "He told me …". Useless. Your managers are there to manage, to make things happen. They are not there to report what someone said, or what someone did, back to you. You don't need a manager to tell you that. They either know themselves or they do not know.

SEEING WHAT OTHERS CAN'T SEE

A very old friend of mine, a Scot called Craig McKinney, set up his own bank in Dublin in 1978. Woodchester specialised in leasing office equipment. It became the biggest lender to the motor industry, which included leasing to the car buyers.

Craig, a real entrepreneur, spotted a small sleepy bank for sale in Dublin, Trinity Bank, owned by a UK bank. Craig wanted Trinity Bank's client book so he could lease more cars to the clients.

But when looking over Trinity's books, he spotted that the property was included. This was a very nice building in the centre of Dublin. It was valued in the company's books at 50% of its market value.

Craig bought the bank. He moved the entire Trinity Bank operation to his own headquarters a quarter of a mile up the road. Soon after, he sold the bank's old premises at market value and made some serious money.

It is not the deal, or the product, or the problem that changes, it is simply how you look at it. Perspective matters. There is more than one way to look at everything. Ultimately what you think is what matters.

11: A FOOT IN THE DOOR

The building services budget was aligned to the size of the business premises. However, despite the amount of money involved, senior managers were reluctant to deal with the building services contract. When we arrived in meetings, in what we called our Smurfit gear, more often than not we would be dealing with middle management. We felt they resented us. There was a constant low-level war, due to us being different. We were the harbingers of change.

Our suits and manner grated on a lot of these middle managers. Sometimes someone would leap up, happy to see at last the industry was getting a well-needed shake up, happy to see we were taking it seriously and professionally. But, more often than not, we alienated them. Normally, we would only meet the top guy in the last meeting. We were making money and we were doing all right, but we were nobody. We were not known. We needed someone who spoke the language, who was known and accepted in the industry.

Owners did not make the cover of magazines working in the building services business. The industry flew under the radar. We needed a foot in the door. We came across a solution: a woman called Mary Stevens. She was very well-known in the building services world. When I met with her, she wanted a share of the business. We gave her 25 per cent.

Stevens' arrival in 1982 brought us more business. Expansion and relative success brought with it two issues. We had recently changed to paying weekly wages by cheque, over the protestations of everyone. Next, I wanted to change to fortnightly wages, and I wanted to get an ICL computer to deal with the wages. Others in the company balked at these changes, warning that the union would cause trouble. My take was to make the change to fortnightly payment, then worry about the union. Better to have the problem after we had done it, rather than before. We were new, so we had to be careful to set the right precedent. We could not be overawed by the union.

This we did. The union, rather than becoming more involved, became less involved. They settled for warning us by phone, rather than in person. They were content to be seen to do something, rather than actually doing something.

Next up was the computer. At meeting after meeting, the other board members voted against it. Eventually, I went out and bought one anyway. They confronted me. I told them I had voted to buy the computer, so I had bought it. They never mentioned it to me again. This confirmed I was in charge. They did not have the courage of their convictions.

AnCo, the government training and employment agency and predecessor of FÁS, began to give us problems. AnCo was a huge customer for us so this was worrying. The board of AnCo was made up mostly of union officials. One man in particular kept asking me why I was "changing everything". I told him I was modernising.

I was called into a meeting with their board on some pretext or another. Effectively, I was being called before the headmaster, to explain my behaviour. I listened to their concerns. I asked them to confirm they were asking me not to computerise or modernise. Luckily, I was always one for studying the lie of the land. On my way up to the meeting, I had walked through the AnCo offices; every single desk had a computer, every single desk. This was in 1984.

I asked the AnCo director, "Are you, an employment agency with a computer on every desk, really asking me not to modernise or computerise my business?".

Once I adopted this approach, they backed down. They started to parrot the same old lines about not wanting to cause any trouble. They seemed to have just been chancing their arm. I suspect the computer was not the real issue. I was free to modernise the business. This meant the business stayed current and kept moving forward. Looking back, it's obvious that not to computerise would have been like fighting the wind, but it was seen as a big deal then. Computers were new. Not a lot of people were using them yet. We needed them for the huge payroll we had. Fighting progress is rarely a good idea, nor often very successful.

Next on the agenda was a new premises. I wanted to buy a place in Harold's Cross, as we had outgrown our place in Camden Street. Once again, nobody in the company wanted to buy the place. I patiently explained it was the business buying the place, not us. They relented after much persuasion.

Bearing in mind what we had learned from the vacuum cleaners, we implemented systems ensuring that when a manager called in to any of the customers, he or she would leave a note informing the relevant employees everything had been looked at. We printed cards for the managers and supervisors to leave signed on the customer's desk day or night. Silence is never a good thing in any business. Regular checks allow you to praise and teach in equal measure. It helps the business to grow and improve all the time. We eschewed the normal complaints book most service companies had for a comments book. This changed the tone of what was written and ended up being a real morale boost for the employees as people tended to write good things.

And, of course, we had checklists for every task in every job. A business without checklists is not performing to its potential. Checklists enable employees to trust themselves; they enable you to trust the staff; most of all they are essential to provide quality. Checklists are absolutely essential. If you don't have them, you are underperforming.

We had won some big contracts by this stage. We had the contract for St James's Hospital and University College Dublin. Guinness Brewery was probably our most high profile. In those days, Guinness Brewery was an antiquated business, albeit a successful one. It had ancient work practices, ancient facilities and was very inefficient.

We were brought in by the management to replace Guinness Brewery's own staff. From the day we moved in, working every day, it took us two months to get the streets and walkways clean. In hindsight, I think, the management brought us in as a modernisation Trojan horse. The Guinness Brewery office cleaners all had had their contracts bought out with very favourable terms.

I could see what they were doing: using us and our employees as a test case. We were advised at tender that Guinness Brewery was a union-only company. Guinness had to know if we could cope with this. We agreed our Guinness Brewery employees would be unionised. In my opinion, we would never been awarded the contracts otherwise. This was always about more than a cleaning contract. Guinness Brewery needed to outsource more of its services to move forward and improve its competitiveness.

We were happy enough to join the union on the bigger sites: St James's Hospital, University College Dublin and Guinness Brewery. It helped legitimise our business in the eyes of other unionised potential customers, and probably led to more contracts. The unions were also happy. They got their subs or fees at base; they let us police the collection of their money and the dubious enforcement of union membership.

As we entered 1987, we had had some problems but nothing major. We were Guinness Brewery's wedge. It was at the beginning of a trend. Government departments and big business led the way. Many of these departments and big businesses thought that they could contract out their problems. They wanted to pay below what was acceptable, expecting companies like ours to magically make this work. They would refuse our employees access to a cloakroom, a storage cupboard and sometimes even running water. They would tell us that these things were not their problem anymore. I used to get this attitude a lot; the belief that outsourcing services was a magical process that negated business realities. The government departments were the worst. These departments expected voodoo accounting to enable them to get toilets and offices cleaned for next to nothing. The unions collected their dues at base, from employees' pay cheques. I believe this meant they were never very motivated. In my opinion, they were less motivated because they could sit in their offices and get their dues. They never had to sell their service.

12: THE 'GUINNESS FIVER'

We worked in Guinness Brewery for the next 20 years, from 1984 to 2004. Our industrial cleaners maintained the yards, the walkways and the hop stores. The Brewery was essentially a food business, so there was a lot of serious cleaning to be done. We made our business more transparent, so the Brewery management could trust us, and see how things worked. In 1988, the Brewery bought out its own industrial cleaners' contracts. It got rid of 24 industrial cleaners and we replaced them with eight people. I would not be telling you a lie if I said the place improved six-fold in two months. This was not magic. Most of the employees bought out had been refugees from long-closed departments. Few had real job titles or genuine responsibilities. Using contract labour, the Brewery was able to increase the number of real hours worked.

Things were moving: we began to pick up more contracts in the Brewery. For example, we took over a two-man department entitled 'furniture removal' – two men who moved the furniture around. We also provided laboratory assistants. We were growing one department at a time.

As our dealings with the Brewery grew, people began to notice. My old employer, Enright, was given a small contract in a bid to keep us honest. The Brewery management wanted to demonstrate that we were not a shoo-in for every contract.

Enright immediately had problems with bringing employees in at 6am. We had instituted this change when we arrived. Before our arrival, employees came in at 5pm or 6pm in the evening. Evening starts were much more difficult to manage, and also led to poorer standards. Every week, when Friday evening rolled around, the employees wanted to be finished for the weekend, to be in the pub with their friends, rather than on their way into work. To overcome their supposed problem, Enright decided to pay their employees an extra £5 to come in at 6am.

Once their employees were getting this extra fiver, the Guinness Brewery branch of the union decided our employees should have it too. I was asked by the Brewery management what I thought about the fiver. I explained simply I was not going to pay it, nor was it included in our pricing. We had already been to the Labour Court to agree a set rate for the contract service sector in Dublin; Guinness was not a special case. The 'Guinness fiver' is what I called it every time I mentioned it, to emphasise it was not something being paid anywhere else. The Guinness fiver. I told the Brewery it was the only company in the whole country that would have to pay this fiver for outsourcing. I suggested to them this was not justifiable.

The union seemed to be using this issue in a roundabout way to attack the Brewery for the increase in outside contracting and to re-affirm its dominance over the company, its workforce and management. The Brewery management understood there was little point in outsourcing without cost-savings. I advised that we wait and see what was next.

The union was threatening to bring the contract services staff out on strike. It was not interested in bringing everyone out on strike at this stage; it was only testing the waters for potential future battles. Our employees were being used as a test case in a proxy war. It was now a case of wait and see who would blink first.

Ironically, and crucially, we had been a signatory on a Labour Court-validated pay agreement a few months before, alongside the union. Together with five other companies, we had agreed a minimum wage for contract service workers. Clients had been using 'bucket and mop' businesses as a way to drive down the hourly rate they paid, driving it below what was acceptable or workable. We needed the minimum wage for a cleaner to be set at a reasonable rate. Together, we all decided we would register an agreed increased rate of pay in the Labour Court. A committee was set up. Representatives of the big six building services companies, as well as the union, were all on the committee. We ended up with a rate of pay validated by the Labour Court. We attached this Labour Court ruling on all affected contracts to avoid any argument. Together with the union, we put a notice in the daily newspapers. The six companies were all named. This proved we could all do business together when we needed to, even when our interests diverged.

Now I was being pitted against the union. I believe the union saw opportunity in the unexpected arrival of outside building service contractors. It enabled them to deal with large labour forces, rather than small family cleaning firms. The unions were making their pitch for the contract workers. With the growth of the building services industry in unionised businesses, hospitals, semi-State bodies, everybody was forced to play with the unions.

The Brewery management was reluctant to become embroiled in an industrial dispute. But they appeared relatively content with how I was dealing with it. The CEO trusting me was the single biggest factor in how things turned out. This trust gave me room to manoeuvre. The contracting out of business services as a cost-cutting measure was the beginning for the Brewery. It wanted to make itself more competitive against other breweries such as Heineken.

The union had a legal obligation to give us seven days' notice in the event of industrial action. It did so, with a hand-delivered letter, during a meeting in the Irish Business and Employers' Confederation (IBEC) offices with the union. I broke the situation down for the union guys and explained how our company and the Brewery were in the middle of a contract with a year or two left to run. We could not afford to bear the cost of an extra fiver on everyone's wage. "There would be no fiver", I told them. The next move was theirs.

I also explained the long and laborious process needed to shut down a brewery, akin to shutting down a furnace. Once it was put in motion, they would have to strike. The shutting-down process was irreversible: the brewery systems took seven days to shut down and another seven to come back up. The union people left the meeting extremely annoyed. I told the Brewery management what was in the letter and they in turn warned me, "Guinness does not go on strike" and "Guinness has never had a strike". I counselled that we hold our nerve a little while longer.

Meanwhile Salmon, a senior union official on the Brewery site, had been in to see management and had made some slanderous statements against my name. This was a mistake on his part. The wrong move. Salmon was not to know it, but his attack weakened the union position and gave us the initiative. He had threatened an all-out strike for the first time and he slandered me; from this, I formulated a plan.

After our minimum wage agreement, the union had taken out an ad in an Irish national newspaper celebrating and informing people of our agreement. In the ad, it had listed its own name as well as the six other signatories. I still had a copy of the ad. I photocopied it and sent it to the Brewery management who, upon seeing it, called Salmon back in.

"How", they asked, "How has Professional Contract Services gone from someone who you partnered with to increase the rate of pay in the building services sector to someone you now hold in such low regard?".

Salmon said that he had a letter that proved all accusations. How a letter could prove untruths was a mystery to me. Management asked him for the letter. Needless to say, it was never produced. Another strategic error.

I sought legal counsel over the defamation of my character. I was informed that union officials' statutory immunity from legal action had just been lifted. I do not think Salmon was aware of this. I told the Brewery that I intended to serve Salmon with a summons for slander. He was not expecting the summons and was shocked.

Less than an hour after the summons, I got a phone call. The Brewery PR man told me how upset Salmon was. Incredible the whole dance. What was the Brewery PR man doing talking to me about how upset Salmon was? I claimed to be more upset. I was a 29-year-old just starting out. And now I was being slandered by people I had recently stood shoulder to shoulder with.

The main thrust of my argument was that this was a personal issue between Salmon and myself. I also stressed that I was prepared to go the whole hog. I was looking to isolate Salmon and put him under pressure. By then, I had everybody's attention. The Brewery moved to separate the issues by emphasising the slander was between McCarthy and Salmon but never backed down from what Salmon had said.

I met a Brewery representative in town. The deadline for the brewery shutdown was looming. Once the shutdown was started, it was irrevocable. The representative told me that Salmon was uncomfortable with the summons. I told the guy, "I'm going to court". He suggested maybe I had won already, that I did not need to keep going.

I stalled, "I am feeling personally aggrieved. My business is being damaged. No one should be allowed do what he did just because he has a position of power. I am going to court so he won't do this again".

Surprised, he went back to the union. All the while, the pressure built on Salmon. The Brewery guy came back to me and said this had to end somewhere. Eventually, I told him, "I want Salmon to stay out of the way, unless there is a legitimate grievance. I do not want any more union posturing at my company's expense. And remind Salmon that the summons has no time limit and can be acted upon in the future".

The threat of the strike was lifted with 24 hours to go to the deadline. This was the end of the matter and, for the next few years, we both benefitted from the arrangement. The union got plenty of new members who had no real say on whether they joined or not. We had a firm foothold in the Brewery and had gained their respect. We picked up many more contracts there: the postal service, customer service, laboratory. The fact we stayed there for 20 years itself speaks volumes. It is practically unheard of in the building services industry to stay anywhere that long. Only when Diageo bought Guinness out and instituted a companywide review did we begin to see the end. We still lasted another four or five years.

It is important to focus on what happened in this story. This is not a cautionary tale about unions one way or the other. It is about standing alone as an entrepreneur. Be prepared to fight for what you believe in. You may not see it coming, but there is always a battle when you disturb the *status quo*. Do not expect anyone to help you out. First, you must prove to them and yourself that you are capable of fighting. They always judge you on your past record. That is how they will decide whether to trust you. Do you do what you say you will, or are you a soft touch? Be prepared to fight.

13: JUST DO IT

In 1989, London was closer by air to Dublin than Limerick or Cork was by road. London had much more opportunity. Opening a business in London had been bandied about by various Dublin building service companies for a while. I liked the idea and was looking to get over there.

Whilst away on holiday, I met a woman working for a property services company, a big company operating multi-storey buildings in and around London. She promised me that, if anything ever came up, she would give me a shout. All I gave her was my card. No harm in asking. Soon after the holiday, she rang me up telling me there was trouble brewing with one of their contractors. The contract, worth around £425,000, was going to be put up for tender soon.

I went over to London to scout the place and walk the city streets. Asking around, I discovered a business in Kensington that would answer phones and redirect mail. I gave my contact the address in Kensington, telling her we would be moving our office closer to the building very soon. Of course, I also told her I would like to be considered for the tender.

All six tendering companies were invited by building services for a walkthrough. They wanted to make a quick decision. After the walkthrough, I asked for a meeting with Steve James, the director of building services, who had brought us around. The ultimate decision was his. This has always been my way. Hold off until you know everything the customer wants. Then, and only then, make your pitch. Hope that no one else has thought of asking to meet the guy. Make sure everything the customer talks about is contained in the pitch.

Like I discovered as a child: find out what your customer wants. Find out what your customer wants and give it to them. Simple and straightforward.

I went to listen to Steve James and to find out what he wanted. Primarily, Steve James wanted to minimise any disruption during the changeover. He was very worried about getting any hassle from the high profile clients in the building: JP Morgan, Bank of America and so on. The previous contractor had given him very short notice. The first question he asked me was how I would go about starting the contract. I acted like I had not heard the question and asked him what the budget was, chancing my arm. Without hesitation, he told me £425,000. I've never been sure if he was onto me, or simply not worried about me knowing. No harm in asking, right?

I told him we had done two sensitive handovers before. Both for high profile companies in Dublin. Putting it all together, I answered, "We'll go into the building eight or nine days before the handover, learning the building, letting people get used to seeing our faces, anticipating any issues before they arise. We'll run the building from the inside rather than our own office".

James did not know we had no office in London. He only heard that I had dealt comprehensively with all his concerns. Again, see the negative of having no office turned into a positive by offering to have our office inside the building. James loved the idea and we immediately began talking logistics. James assured me he could arrange for our basement office to have outside telephone lines. He offered to pay for them. Like the assumed close with the photocopier, we were already discussing the job as if we had got it.

Sure enough, we got the contract. Once it was signed, the next thing was to raise capital to absorb initial expenses. I needed £30,000. I could have taken the £30,000 from the Dublin business but my policy has always been every part of the business must be self-sustaining, must pay its own way. The two Irish banks in London balked at the amount. It was too little. They had no interest.

Back in Dublin, I got the number of someone I vaguely knew who had recently moved to Bank of Ireland in London. When we met in London, he showed up smoking a big cigar: all London, fair play to him. He said that £30,000 was no bother. He was happy an Irish firm had won such a big job in Moorgate in the City of London.

One of the great things about working in London, particularly the office blocks, was that, on top of the initial deal for a building, we would make nearly as much again on additional contracts with individual businesses. They all needed or wanted offices and boardrooms cleaned and renovated. More often than not they would take us with them when they left and the replacement tenant also would take us on. These deals were worth a fortune to us and were all done without market research or consultants. It was a pleasure working with these businesses. I never had to chase the money. People always paid on time in the City and I felt it was a good place to do business.

Our first address was on beautiful London Wall, London. Six months later, we moved to a proper office on Liverpool Street. We stayed there 20 years. I have been asked many times to tell this story. I always simply tell the truth, "I walked around London for a few days to get the lie of the land, I tendered for a contract and made the sale".

Nothing complicated: all attainable through hard work. What has surprised me through the years is how dissatisfied people are with this answer. Their eyes glaze over and they stop listening. I began to realise that they want to hear about magic. They want to hear entrepreneurial fairy tales. They want me to tell them I met someone in a bar, we got drunk and I was given the business. When all they hear is hard work and clear thinking, they tune out because they can do these things themselves.

People seem to want something out of the ordinary to have happened, that the business fell into my lap. In short, they want to hear I was lucky. Luck is a vague misty idea nobody fully understands. The only thing people understand is that they personally are not lucky. This story has no lessons for them because they have no luck.

Maybe they are right. Maybe I was lucky. If I was lucky, I was lucky because I did it. I was lucky because I did something. I was lucky because I bought the ticket to London. Hard work and lots of thinking are the magic. There is nothing else. Alchemy in business stems from toil and contemplation. Taking action causes things to happen.

Who in their right mind would try to open a business in the centre of London? When the idea arrived on my desk, we had nothing in London, so off I went. The first thing we needed was an address, so that was the first thing I got. We had no office, so we used that to our advantage. We had no employees, so we kept on the old employees, at the beginning at least.

I sold the business in the UK in 2008. For 20 years, I had gone over to London twice a month to ensure everything was running smoothly. The businesses in Ireland and England had roughly the same number of employees: 1,200 employees each. In Ireland, we spent a day and a half in one court or another every month, defending what we knew to be bogus claims in some cases. We spent our lives defending ourselves from different cases taken by the unions. In the UK, we ran the business the exact same way and we never had any problems: none. In Ireland, our employer's liability insurance was £125,000, in England £20,000. This was a huge discrepancy and indicates the more litigious culture in Ireland.

I got the business in the UK because I bought the ticket. I got it because I went. I got it because I just did it. Nike has been telling us for years: 'Just do it'. Well, I just did. We went over there with nothing, with lots of excuses not to go if we wanted. That never mattered though. That is something for others to worry about. We went over there to do it.

A guy wins the lottery, not because he is lucky, but because he bought a ticket. Somebody always wins the lottery, but only because they have bought a ticket.

FINDING THE POSITIVE IN THE NEGATIVE

"Turn the negative into a positive" is a phrase you meet everywhere – but what does it mean in practice?

Turning the negative into a positive is a skill. Like any skill mentioned in this book, it can be learned by anyone. For some people, it comes easier than for others, but it can be learned and used by all.

When you apply this skill to your own life, to your business or to your job, you are not magicking away the negative. You are simply looking at it in a clear manner, seeking to find the positive in the negative. If a negative exists, there must be a positive. The skill lies in finding it. You do not need to deny the existence of the negative, but you must believe that you will find the positive.

Believing the positive exists is the first step. It is a technique that must be practised. It is more difficult at the beginning, although some people get it straight away. Consider the example of the half-empty glass: if anything is half-empty, it stands to reason it also must be half-full.

In the story of the Omega photocopiers, the negative was that the copier was unable to deal with high volume and often went on fire. But therein also lay the positive: the copier was able to deal with lower volume and provide better quality than other low volume copiers. So why not pitch it against other lower volume machines?

The solution was not difficult. However, this way of thinking is not what is taught in schools or at work. People's minds are used to honing in on and dwelling on the negative. We have not been taught to derive a positive from a problem or a difficulty. We have been taught that negative events are end-of-the-line scenarios rather than the beginning of, or springboard to, something else.

Some of the old stationery in Henry Jackson was over 15 years old; some of it was rusted or dried up. There was a huge amount of it. Apparently, nobody wanted it. Nobody could see past these negatives.

But because a lot of it was almost worthless, this provided the positive: we could sell it for very little. We are not changing what is in the glass; we are merely looking at it differently. When I looked at the huge amounts of surplus stock, coupled with the low price, I realised that I could offer someone an attractive deal. And I have to say, Petticoat Lane played its part too. It was a rough place, with even rougher business practices. There were no guarantees once money had changed hands. This was another positive as it meant that once the deal had gone through, there would be no comebacks.

The magic of actually getting out there and doing it needs to be liberally sprinkled on everything. Action is everything. Every single thing that happens in this book, including the book itself, has come about through thought and action.

None of this is weird stuff, none of this is magic, all of it is simply thinking in a different way. The knack is to remember that you have been taught your whole life to regard a negative as something to be feared and avoided. When you next encounter a problem or a perceived negative, remember to look for the positive. Spin the facts around, as you would a mental carousel. If it does not come immediately, give yourself a break, walk away, do something else. The positive is in there and it will reveal itself to you in time. You will see it then.

14: EXPECT THE UNEXPECTED

Running a business is a test of every skill you have. When you open your own business, you can find yourself having to learn about grease traps one minute, pigeons' feeding habits the next. Here are two issues we did not see coming, but are part of a larger tapestry of unexpected events that any entrepreneur has to deal with and think their way out of.

THE EMBASSY

The embassy was a difficult contract due to the strict security arrangements. People had to be thoroughly vetted well in advance. If an employee was absent or somebody quit, we could not replace them on short notice. To overcome this, we had a special agreement with our embassy employees, they would make up the shortfall, and do the extra work if someone was absent. The embassy building manager was not interested in our problems; he just wanted his building cleaned and maintained.

Despite all this, it was a high profile client and we were happy to have it. There were always a lot of soldiers to ensure the place was well guarded.

One Saturday morning, our manager got in contact with us. There had been a situation at the embassy we needed to deal with. I went there immediately to speak to the supervisor.

The soldiers on guard had used our six employees as mock terrorist intruders, as part of a secret training drill. Our employees were captured, put up against a wall, tied up and held captive by fully armed soldiers. Eventually, they were untied and released. They had had the life frightened out of them. Nobody on our side knew about this plan, so there was terror. I went in to speak to the authorities in the embassy.

They told me I was making too big a deal of it. I went through the usual, "I am not making a big deal of anything". I explained these people were in my employment; that, in the course of their work, they had been taken hostage; nobody had been asked or informed; on reflection, the whole thing stank. There was an arrogance about it that has always stuck in my throat.

After the weekend, the soldiers went around to our employees, gave them a box of chocolates and chatted to them. The employees were all proud to work in the embassy and let it go, although the relationship between us and the embassy never really recovered. I was concerned my employees would take a claim against us or the embassy. Nothing ever transpired. It was a different world then; nowadays, it would be around the world in a heartbeat on Twitter.

The story is a good insight into how people regarded building service employees and people who did that type of work. The embassy was not alone in thinking that our employees could be treated differently. Businesses generally thought these people were lucky to have a job. A lot of it was down to companies having contracted out the work. And having contracted out the work, many businesses wanted to forget about the whole thing.

This attitude was everywhere in the 1980s. Clients would not provide anywhere for our employees to hang their coats or keep their equipment, or they would not give them access to running water. This became such an issue that we developed a pre-start system. Once the contract was signed, we would go into the business and have a list of questions for the client to answer. Show me the plugs, running water, cloak room: the necessities. Clients would be amazed we were doing this. They would tell us that, if they had known that our employees were going to need a cupboard or running water, then they would not have signed the contract. "We don't charge you for electricity" was the prevailing attitude of the time. You have to be prepared to stand up for yourself. The 'customer is always right' mantra does not apply if the customer is being completely unreasonable.

THE TAX-FREE ALLOWANCE

I began work in a world that no longer exists. I have worked and lived through massive changes in work, work practices and work forces. Perhaps nowhere is the change more noticeable than in the working life of women. During the 1960s and 1970s, the husband controlled both tax-free allowances. You could say the husband owned his wife's tax-free allowance. If a woman wanted to use her allowance in her job, she would have been told in the tax office, "You had better go and talk to your husband". Not good.

When we started Professional Contract Services, we found it difficult to employ people. There were issues regarding part-time tax rates. A lot of our employees were women and they could not get access to their tax-free allowance. This was the way it was, with regards to part-time work, in the late 1970s in Ireland. As well as this, if you were working under 20 hours a week, you were not really on the Revenue's radar yet. The government then decided enough was enough and declared they wanted part-time workers to pay tax like everyone else.

Not paying tax was one issue. The other issue was that husbands were claiming their wives' tax-free allowance. Often, even if the wife wanted the allowance back, the husband would not sign it back. A lot of these women were fed up being at home. In those days, there wasn't much a woman could do on her own in Ireland. Women could not really go into a bar on their own – well, they could, but they seldom did. The café culture was only beginning and tended to be mostly in the city. More than any of this though, being stuck in the house was not acceptable to women any longer. A lot of them had no other life besides the home and the family: work was a way to get out, and a whole lot more. The husband would bring home the pay packet and would hand over what he thought was needed. Rarely was there much money for the woman herself. She was 'rewarded' with a drink or two in the lounge on a Sunday night. Our married female employees struggled to get their tax-free allowance off their husbands. This was inhibiting our ability to employ the right people.

I did not want to start with a payroll tax system that was going to come back on us later. I went to see the Revenue and told them what they already knew about the marital tax-free allowance. We worked out a deal that, for every £15 we paid our employees, we would give the Revenue £3. This covered the social welfare 'stamp' as well. The stamp allowed people to obtain assistance from the social welfare department. We did this to enable our employees to work, pay tax legally and to avoid any trouble for our company. The people who were coming into our place for jobs often were unsure where they stood tax-wise, and thus were very reluctant to work.

A lady used to come in regularly. She would ask "Are there any little jobs? Cash in the hand?". She had the receptionist persecuted. Before I struck the deal with the Revenue, I had always told her "No". I'd told her many times but she'd persevered. When I came back from the Revenue with the deal, I was able to offer her a job at £12 'into the hand'. Little did she know she was paying tax. She took this job and worked with us without any bother.

We were offering people £12 take-home pay; we told them the company paid the tax. If they wanted to pay their own tax, then we offered £15, minus the tax and plus their allowance. Ninety per cent of the employees chose to take the £12. 'Into the hand' was the second most important thing. The most important thing was they did not need to tell their husbands. They could go off out to work without letting on or causing a fuss. Without having to ask the husband for anything.

This went on for a couple of years. Eventually, we were notified that the Revenue was going to change the tax system. Everyone was warned. Everyone was told and, because of this, the changeover was a success. Some employees left. But most husbands gave back or relinquished control over the allowance. There had been a national conversation about it.

When we got all the tax certificates, we reconciled everybody's tax. Most people ended up paying no tax, the rest paid less tax than before. Nobody needed to pay as much as £3 anymore. All our employees got an effective pay rise when the changeover happened. Between the tax, women not having control of their own financial affairs and part-time workers not being part of the tax system, it was a bewildering scenario. There was so much wrong with it, but it was a reflection of the times.

The embassy and the tax-free allowance are just two examples of issues we dealt with over the years, often issues we had not anticipated, when we had to improvise solutions.

Business really is real life. Running a business includes everything. You need to think your way out of these trials. But I would be lying if I did not admit I relished these challenges. I enjoyed them. Thinking and solving problems is an entrepreneur's lifeblood.

15: REDUNDANCY & REBIRTH

According to the *European Employment Rights Act, 1996,* an employee is dismissed by reason of redundancy if the dismissal is wholly or mainly attributable to the fact that the employer ceases to carry on the business in which the employee was employed, or ceases to carry on that business in the place where the employee was employed. A redundancy also will occur when the business need for employees to carry out a particular kind of work has ceased or diminished.

You do not become redundant; your job does. Of course, subtle definitions do not compensate for the shock of losing your job; after all, it was a way of life for you, often alongside good friends who now may drift to a different path.

However, there are many who say redundancy has been the best thing that ever happened to them, who are now enjoying great success. They are doing something they really like, operating at their own pace, making their own decisions and earning a lot more money for themselves and their family. Most importantly of all, they will never let the perceived horror of redundancy happen to them again. If you have been made redundant, you must grasp the opportunity this change has provided you with.

Ask yourself, "Has this redundancy presented me with a chance to tackle that notion I have always flirted with? The secret idea of working for myself, a chance for change? A chance to do something new with the freedom that self-employment brings?".

Of course it has. It has given you an opportunity, but you have to take it. I know many who have taken the leap, and I must say I know not one who has gone back.

For those who believe, no proof is necessary.

For those who do not believe, no proof will suffice.

STARTING YOUR OWN BUSINESS

When I talk to people about redundancy, I like to talk to them about opening their own business and some of the things they need to think about before they do.

Businesses don't make money, people do. So by following this through, you start with the most important person: yourself.

You need to ask yourself what is it you want. What type of life do you envisage:

o Do you envisage a full-time job?

o Do you imagine working four hours per day?

o Do you want to do the work yourself?

o Do you want to earn lots of money?

o Do you want to work on your own?

o Do you want to include your family in a business you can expand?

o Do you understand that you must love what you do? (This is critical)

o Is it management opportunities you are looking for?

o Can you find something that can match the experience you already have?

o Do you want a complete change of career?

o Do you want to work locally?

Once you have answered these questions honestly to yourself, you might think about talking to someone about your idea.

Do not talk to the following:

o The guy or girl down in the club or the pub.

o Someone who has not achieved much in life themselves.

o Someone who is forcing you to do what they believe you should do (their great idea).

o Someone who gets upset when you do not follow their advice.

Simply put; only speak to those who have achieved.

Once you have answered these questions, then it is the time to talk to the bank:

o Explain your position.

o Tell them what you want to achieve.

o Talk to them about why you have chosen to become an entrepreneur.

Explain your general idea and plan. You are in the bank to find out how much you will be able to borrow, what kind of credit facility is available. After you leave, you will have a general idea of what you can do, how much funds are available.

There are a couple of unspoken rules to being an entrepreneur. These are well explained in a book called *The Four Agreements*, based on the writings of Don Migel Ruiz:

o **Be impeccable with your word.** Do not speak ill of yourself or others. There is no good to be had from using your word to poison your own life, or the lives of those around you.

o **Don't take anything personally.** People have their own problems. You cannot control what they do. Relinquish any anxiety you have over what others feel about you.

Free yourself from the shackles of gossip and innuendo.
They speak and think only of themselves, no matter what
they say or do.

o **Don't make assumptions.** Be specific in question, in
answer and in action. This is beautiful. This will change
your life. Find out exactly what you are communicating
about, let there be no doubt.

o **Always do your best**. Sounds simple right? If you do
your best, you leave nothing behind to dwell on in the
future. Whatever your best is, give it to whatever you are
doing. Why are you saving something? This is the main
act.

As you can see these are agreements with yourself. One other I
might add from my own experience is to be prepared to be
unpopular.

In addition:

o To be an entrepreneur, you must work like one: hard.

o Shake off old habits: it's a new world and a different one.

o You will be told often it cannot be done – then you must
go and do it.

o You cannot ever be a spectator – you must be a player.

o You do not want to be the dancer – you have got to be the
dance.

You must begin to develop the thinking habits we have
discussed, those of an entrepreneur:

o Everything you see around you was once a thought; now
take time, look around, see and think.

o Think and act positively; they must work together.
Action is always required – only thinking positive, that's
for dreamers.

o A car design begins with a thought; it is put on paper and then built. The architect, the clothes designer, the glass blower, they all begin their process with a thought.

o An artist visualizes the picture, then paints it. Action is always required: YOURS!

When is the right time to make this leap? When you are ready is the right time:

o Ray Kroc started at 52 years old and expanded McDonalds to 35,000 outlets worldwide.

o Mark Zuckerberg founded Facebook aged 20. When he was 26 years old, his net worth was $15 billion.

Once more simply:

o **What do you want?** Decide who you should talk to. Start to research opportunities. Look beyond the idea, think specifics. Give yourself a timeframe to make a decision.

o **Select three opportunities that meet your personal requirements:** Research these diligently and honestly.

o **Bank:** Get finance broadly agreed in advance.

o **Remember you must love what you are about to do:** Now make a decision.

Good luck. Remember to love whatever you do.

THE SEASONING PRINCIPLE

When I was a 12-year-old lad, a regular chore given to me by my mother was to collect the meat from the butcher shop. When collecting the meat, the butcher would ask if I required seasoning, I always said "Yes", although at the time, I never knew what seasoning was. Later, I learnt that seasoning was a 50/50 mixture of salt and pepper that flavoured and spiced the meat. I became a lover of this seasoning although I have never liked salt, and pepper is just horrible. What became clear to me was that, accidentally or otherwise, the butcher had made a third product called seasoning. Two completely different tastes, that when mixed together, tasted nothing like the two original ingredients.

For a partnership to work well, it has to be like seasoning. When pepper partners salt, it is no longer pepper and *vice versa*. You can tell from the taste of the seasoning that neither ever tries to be the other and so together they become a success. When two people decide that marriage or a business partnership is for them, it would be a great start to their new partnership in life if they could grasp this seasoning principle. Both partners must be mindful they will not be the individuals they once were; they are now a partnership, something new. If one tries to dominate or overpower the other, then the partnership cannot and will not work. We spend so much time looking and finding the ideal partner, we love what we see, only to then turn around and spend the rest of our life trying to change them.

In the seasoning model, pepper allows salt to be salt; salt allows pepper to be pepper; and together they make a very successful partnership. Salt and pepper are individuals no more, they no longer exist separately.

Learn this seasoning model and watch how much happier you become.

16: CHALLENGES

Here are five simple challenges that will bring immediate results.

CHALLENGE 1

OK, let's start with an obvious one that we all like to avoid. When you decided to invest in a pension, did you just hand a cheque to a broker or a consultant and get no information of the pension breakdown? I know you did, you know you did. Go and find out what kind of pension plan you have. Follow the investigation to the end:

- o How much of the money you have invested is still there?
- o What is that money doing at the moment?
- o What monthly or annual charges and fees do you pay?
- o What is the value of the pension plan?
- o What percentage does your broker get?
- o How much money is that?

Then when you have asked all the above, do not believe or accept any of the answers? Ask for proof. To find out the truth, tell your broker, or whomever, that you want to cash your policy today. Ask them how much they will give you. Ask them the encashment value. Repeat your question until you get the encashment value. They will give you every single other type of value possible: do not settle for less than the current encashment value. Ask to see all the information. Once you have the information in front of you, confirm how much you are entitled to. Most likely, you will discover that the value is somewhat less than you expected.

This is useful to find out the reality of your financial situation. Similarly, it teaches you the important skill of not believing everything you are told, especially just because you are being told by people the world calls 'professionals'. Professionals expect people to believe everything they tell you without question. Financial institutions, in particular, like giving you answers to questions you did not ask. Stick to your questions. Do not be intimidated. An entrepreneur must make up their own mind. An entrepreneur cannot trust their lawyer or their accountant without fully understanding the issue themselves.

Taking this idea further, through the analysis and understanding of accepted practices, efficiency and leanness can be found. Fat or excess can be exposed and eliminated. In short, money can be saved. Why does your accountant or your lawyer do things the way they do? Is there a cheaper and / or a better way? These are questions you need to know the answer to.

On any level, believing what you are told simply because someone is a professional is inadvisable and hazardous. Why are you afraid to cause a fuss? It is your pension, after all.

CHALLENGE 2

Get up early and contemplate. Rise no later than 7.30am.

This is an easy one. The early period of the day, before things really begin to happen, is when an entrepreneur has time to contemplate. This is a vital weapon in the arsenal of any entrepreneur. Give yourself some time in the morning to think over what the day holds and whatever else is on your mind.

If you want to sleep in, win the lottery first.

CHALLENGE 3

Stop poisoning your children with processed food. No fizzy drinks. No junk. Stop convincing yourself that it is OK to feed your kids junk. Stop over-feeding your kids.

Be honest with yourself about how you are influencing your children's diet. Really, who is buying the food? Who is choosing easy-to-make food? Your kids don't buy the food, do they? You do, don't you?

Start small. Do not tell anyone what you are doing. Do not give up.

CHALLENGE 4

Write down five things a partner or a good friend does regularly in one week for you or with you. When the week is finished, give them a note of appreciation. Give people credit. I am talking about not taking people for granted. Most of all though, I am asking you to reflect on what it is your partner does for you. I want you to take the focus off the 'me, me, me' route.

This is particularly important in a partnership or any good relationship. Give people credit. Give your kids credit. They deserve it. Recognise the good in your partner, in your spouse, in your son or daughter. Tell them why what they did helped and pleased you. Put it out there.

CHALLENGE 5

This for all you people out there afraid to say "No". The next time you are asked to do something you do not need or want to do, have the courage to say "No" and give the general reason why. Try this in five tiny situations, see how the result does not harm you and learn it is OK to say "No".

Cause a fuss when you encounter bad service or bad treatment. Complain when it is warranted. Do not be embarrassed. Complain. When you go to the doctor, do not let yourself be shunted out the door dissatisfied. Wherever you are, if you feel you are being unfairly treated, do not stand for it.

Argue. Stand up for yourself. Stop being such a pushover. Why are you letting other people think for you? Why do you not run your own life?

17: ESPECIALLY FOR STUDENTS

This chapter is especially for the many students who feel under pressure to pursue a study / career path not of their liking. Many of you may be following a path that will cause you stress and worry by putting time and energy into something you do not want or love.

My advice is to go and ask your parents for your independence – your life's independence. Independence from future employers; independence from giant multinationals that hire and fire according to market trends; independence from the five-year whims of whatever government has managed to persuade us they are ever so slightly different; independence from the State; independence from redundancy; independence from the mistakes of others; independence with freedom of mind, your OWN mind. This is what you need to be truly yourself.

Some of you may already have your independence. Your parents are genuinely supportive. And perhaps you have long ago decided that following in their footsteps – becoming a doctor, a solicitor, an accountant or an engineer – is your own dream. If so, away you go and do not look back or down. There is no wrong way, so long as the decision is your own.

The greatest gift a parent can give their offspring is their freedom. If you have not been given yours yet, go and ask for it – now.

What to do: Find a college friend in similar circumstances to yourself and agree that both of you will ask your respective parents on the same evening for your independence. Go get it and keep it. Be mindful that your parents may stick their finger in your pie every now and again until they get the whole message. Reassure yourself that this is about you, your independence. If you feel under pressure, if you feel you are being pushed into doing something you don't like, explain to your parents that you would rather pursue your own ideas on life.

As you transition from teenager to adult, parents believe they are helping and can become overzealous in trying to guide their young adult through their studies and onto a career path. They do this honestly and with a pure heart. Gently explain to them that you have other ideas.

It is very difficult for your parents to understand that they do not own you. They have been your guardians through life and your most important teachers. But that is where it stops. It is up to you to assert yourself. It is up to you to understand that the responsibility for your own life lies with you. Maybe because your parents finance your education, you feel that you do not have any choice in what you do. Nothing else could explain the fear that students exhibit in university other than feeling they are responsible for someone other than themselves.

Your life is not about your parents, but about you. Do you want to take your life into your hands? When you are in control of your own life, this is the beginning of finding your own way. The person who has found their own way need not be rich or poor in the bank, for they are rich in life. You can recognise these people very easily: their work is their life and they see no divide. They can be an artist or a football coach; there are no rules. Find these people and talk to them, tell them about your plans and you will find that they will encourage you in every way. Anyone who has their own independence will want you to have yours. Like any great feeling, success is enhanced by sharing it.

Go and ask for your independence. I cannot imagine a life working for someone else. When people love what they do, working hard and putting all the hours they have into what they love comes very easy and this is a vital factor to being successful. It is the greatest feeling in life.

An entrepreneur is an independent soul. A student who comes into the business world not knowing where the parameters or the obstacles are often overcomes them. Young people often do not know but therein lies their greatest strength. Inside your negative lies your positive.

Release yourself from other people's control. Control can manifest itself in many different ways whether in social norms, religious persecution or rules (especially unwritten rules). Avoid, ignore and break through these controls.

The greatest gift parents can give their children is their independence, giving them total freedom to follow their dreams whatever they may be. It's impossible to live someone else's dream. Must the farmer's son be a farmer or the doctor's daughter be a doctor? These dreams belong to the parent and perhaps not to the son or daughter. If parents want to be proud of their children's success, they must give them their independence and the right to choose for themselves.

It's not the end of the world if a young adult, for whatever reason, does not take the university route. Almost all successful entrepreneurs never achieve that level of education: neither

Mark Zuckerberg nor Bill Gates graduated from university. Clearly, there are other routes to success.

And why is it that when a student, after a long hard road of study, finally graduates, they choose to work for large firms? Should the option not be to work for themselves, to be independent, to become entrepreneurs and to make their own decisions? The entrepreneur route should be a consideration for every graduate.

Nothing compares with the feeling of working for yourself. Once you are on that path, you cannot easily be knocked from it. How can you be knocked from the path if the path *is* you? If it is the embodiment of you?

Don't delay, why don't you go and do it now? Ask for your independence. What are you waiting for? Start living your own life.

AFTERWORD: WHY I WROTE THIS BOOK

I have found it very difficult to faithfully explain my thoughts and my thought processes in writing this book. I have always known I wanted to write a book – and now I have. However, my worry has always been I would be misunderstood – or, worse, not understood at all. This is the final chapter in the explanation, and once more I ask you for your attention as I seek to explain who it is I am by telling you one more story.

Becoming an entrepreneur is not something I set out to do. It is still a word I am vaguely uncomfortable with, since I feel it makes starting a business seem unusual or foreign when it is the most natural thing in the world. Working for myself is where my thoughts led me. Being under anyone else's thumb made me feel ill and restricted. I have striven to follow my path, or more accurately I have gone where I felt was the natural place to go.

At the beginning, I never understood I was taking the positive from the negative; I had never really thought like that. Like most of you reading this book, this way of thinking had never occurred to me. Why would it? This left me feeling alone a lot. It also left me feeling quite unhappy, I felt I was different, awkward, I felt apart. I hope that by recounting the following experience to you, I can offer you a spur to begin a life of thought.

Looking back now, I see my life as having two distinct phases. When I began my working life, I did things: sometimes the right thing, sometimes the wrong thing, but I never reflected much on what was going on in my head. I went and did things that felt right. I went where I thought was the right place to go. This served me well enough. What follows is a brief explanation of the day that everything changed for me.

1992 was a year to remember for me: I was not well. I'd lost a great deal of weight. My entire immune system was under attack. I was struggling on many fronts. I looked bad, I was tired a lot, I never held onto a meal very long. I was tested for ME and for a variety of other things, but my condition remained a mystery. My doctor, Dr Doyle, had had some success treating me. However, any time it seemed we were close to a cure, I would crash again. I was never bed-ridden, but there was no normal way of getting through the days.

Dr Doyle had been treating this elusive illness for two years, though he could never give it a name. When people know you are not well and you cannot give them the name of the ailment, they start speculating and talking about the plague and other extremes. This was driving me crazy, the constant speculation. I had a great thought: give it a name myself, shut them up and get some peace. After a little research, I decided to call the monster candida (an irritable bowel type of ailment), although I had been tested for candida and had been assured that I definitely did not have it. Once I named it, I got some peace from my good friends and a lot of jokes. Then I had another thought, I don't know where from, "if I am calling it candida, why not treat it like candida?".

I bought a book on treating candida and started doing exactly that, completely changing my diet. As a young man, weekends and Friday nights were a big part of my life, but the drink had to go. I could never think clearly and drink, it had always disrupted my ability to think for days afterwards.

Next, I went to Dr Doyle and told him what I was going to do. I explained that, if he could live with it, I would do it under his watch. Though none too happy – "Any quack stuff and I will be out of it" – he agreed.

Without my knowledge, my PA, who was up to speed on the issue, had made an appointment for me to visit a stress management consultant, Ryan. I was feeling a lot better, but I agreed to go anyway. On the fourth or fifth visit, I asked Ryan, "Where are we at?". Ryan was a great note-taker but he said he was lost, he felt I should meditate. I asked him to demonstrate how, as I had no idea at all. I practiced this meditation at home with no success.

On my next visit, I explained I needed him to show me there and then. Ryan said he felt that I was blocking something out, not allowing it into my mind. He felt that something was trying to get my attention and he assured me that meditation would help. Having been shown what to do, I relaxed and began.

Some minutes into the meditation, I saw a clapperboard, just like at the beginning of a movie. My impression was that I was being brought into a movie. I went with it. I zoomed first through and beyond the clouds, into a beautiful bright indigo sky.

Next, I saw an eye, a very big, friendly, powerful eye. The eye wanted to show me something; it would be my guide. I agreed. Off we shot into a starry sky. My eyes were the camera. It seemed we were traveling a long way; for some reason, I felt sure it was a very long way. We approached this vortex in the sky, similar to a black hole. Backwards, but head first, we went in. I went on a tour of a terrible place. I became a little anxious. I was reassured I had total control, to take note that this was a very big place.

I saw an endless street of houses unfurled ahead of me, each smoky door guarded. Souls were free to come and go, but they never did; fear had gripped them. Fear now owned them and controlled them. I somehow sensed all this. The faceless guards that stood everywhere were afraid, it was only then I realised that they were afraid of my guide. They understood we knew their bark was a big bluff. Only wisdom, I thought, could conquer here. No soul could leave here, simply because they believed they could not leave. They were afraid; they did what they were told and followed the loudest mouth. They never tested it; there was nobody there to learn from. It was all misery and fear.

I was always aware of the vastness of the place. The mere fact of being there was an ordeal. I sensed epochal suffering, but it was always once removed from me as I had someone with me. It was the roughest, wildest area imaginable but I was never in danger. My guide never shied away from confronting these people; his courage was a shield. His strength scared them. The eternal battle was being waged, but there was never any doubt in my mind about who would triumph.

After a period outside of normal time, my guide asked me if I wanted to leave. I agreed. There was a slight pause, then my guide handed me off to another guide and left. I popped up into this nice sunny day. It was so bright. I felt the elation we all get on a beautiful day. Under my control, we travelled a lot more, to different dimensions, if that's what they were. I would simply think up, then down, left, then right and the response was always instant. I was told more than once I was in complete control. I could return when I felt the urge to do so. I was reminded not to try and take all this in at once, take everything gently, very gently. During this journey, I drifted back to the consultant's room, then back again. The thought here was for me to grasp that I was in two places. It was like I lived in an apartment and I was listening to myself upstairs. I understood that I was in two places at once and always would be. This was when I began to comprehend that I was not dreaming; that I was able to return to myself and then to go back. I was the boss.

My guide urged me to look after my health. Only one solid instruction, more like advice, strong advice: "You have to do this for yourself, everything is up to you. Some people when they are shown these things go crazy, some people ignore it and some simply don't care. The choice will always be yours. Forever".

The guide continued, "You will get comfortable, in time, with yourself and, as you become more aware, the work will always be your own".

Aeons passed as I flew over another wasteland somewhat less barren and less fearful but horrific nonetheless, with aimless people walking around. I flew over historical scenarios. I went back and forth through my own life, where some faces were visible, others were blackened out. Time was not an issue; my sometimes vertical flight exposing various levels up and down. I took in all of this. My comprehension was instantaneous. Eventually, I was made aware that this was the journey of a soul.

On my way back, my guide assured me I had done enough. His final thoughts to me were "Sack this consultant now, never allow anyone to take control of you. Be very wary of the charlatans, dreamers, prophets and shamans of this world. Stay on your own".

Back at the consultant's office, I had a story to tell, along with the message that I would not be using him again. He accepted it fully. He explained himself by saying he had never told me what to do, or counselled me, he had just listened. As a result of what he had heard, he advised me to read *Awareness* by Anthony De Mello. I did. I thoroughly recommend it. It cracks the shell of the egg on the subject of thought and prepares you for a new way of thinking. The awareness comes all of sudden and you never look back.

The sickness left, never to return. I believe alcohol stifles thinking and I have never really drunk again. Maybe two glasses of wine a year, to convince people I am not an alcoholic. Currently, my strongest thoughts arrive in the early morning, when I lie in full contemplation. Weekends are a good time to try it. Awareness, what is it? It's awaking from the day-to-day slumber so many of us live in.

Before this happened to me, I had never really given any thought to thinking. I was never taught anything about thinking in school. There was no conversation about thinking at home. I truly hope that, after reading this book, you will start thinking. It was that day in the stress consultant's office that I first thought about thought. I was still an entrepreneur, but when I understood my thought process, I was an infinitely happier entrepreneur. I started to treat my mind like I would my body. The sciences of the mind only ever seem to be considered when something is broken or damaged. Surely this is the wrong way around?

Nowadays, when I feel myself being attacked, or I feel frustrated, unable to get someone to see my point of view, I like to remind myself of the junkyard dog and the poodle. Whichever you feed grows and thrives. Whichever you starve withers and weakens. When you mix with the right people, positive people, then the poodle grows and strengthens. Use this idea, this technique, to help you survive the slings and arrows of negativity. I carry it around inside me, call upon it whenever I sense the junkyard dog get off its hind legs and begin to threaten. This idea of the two dogs inside all of us, one destructive and rotten, the other creative and clear, is told in many cultures across the world. I find it helps me to remember I can only ever account for myself. I control only my own thoughts. We must remember only our reaction to others is under our control. Whichever beast we choose to give succour to is the one that will inhabit us.

Lastly, I would like to thank you for buying this book. I wanted to give you something other than words, something tangible, something you can feel, smell and hold, something to believe in. The often elusive proof of everything I have written about is the book in your hands; I do not have to utter another word. Although I have had an enormous amount of support from those around me in writing this book, the naysayers have not stopped. I still have to steel myself against their insidious doubts:

- o "I will believe it when I see it."
- o "You will not find it easy – and then you have to publish."
- o "You will never finish it."
- o "Rather you than me."
- o "Where will you get the time?"

And then, of course, when you do succeed, the best one of all, the catch-all: "You got lucky, you were really lucky".

Understand that they will never stop. They are all around us. The naysayers are our friends, our family and often our teachers. Use these doubters to drive yourself forward as I have always done. How dare they tell us it cannot be done. Prove them wrong and, in the end, you will walk tall, real tall.

You must believe in yourself and in your idea, your vision, your business. Throughout this book, throughout history, we have seen examples of this. The times I felt isolated, when I alone saw something, saw a solution or an alternative, people told me I was crazy, told me I was deluded. But look what happened when Ryanair came along and did what Aer Lingus claimed was impossible. And who would ever have thought that buying bottled water would become the norm?

This book is proof that the way of the entrepreneur is paved by results. The entrepreneur likes to achieve things through contemplation and action.

Think. Thinking is the greatest gift we have been given, it is our greatest weapon as we walk along our lives. The mind is the key to a lifetime of fulfilment and contentment, for us and our families.

I have endeavoured to demystify what an entrepreneur does and is. An entrepreneur is not one thing; an entrepreneur is a culmination of all the experiences in this book, as well as lots and lots of thinking. It's never about the money for the entrepreneur.

Good luck. I hope you enjoyed the book. Don't be afraid to read it again. Often the second reading is when the truths and lessons are fully revealed.

Remember just think and do. Think and do.

FRANK McCARTHY

Frank McCarthy was born in 1951, in Dublin, Ireland. His schooling finished as quickly as it started, in 1964, aged 13.

In 1994, he married Sinead Rogers, a designer from the West of Ireland. Sinead had success of her own: a wedding designer, she owned The Bridal Gallery, Dublin and produced a creation for one of the American Kennedy family.

Frank has three children: Rob 27, Meg 13, and Amy 12, all of whom currently are living in Dublin

Frank enjoys a weekly game of golf, and holidaying in his two favourite countries: the USA and France. He also, if he is honest, likes getting embroiled in discussions on anything and everything.

His favourite quote is: "Fear knocked on my door. Faith answered and there was no one there".

His first business venture was Professional Contract Services in 1978. He was then only 27 years old.

Professional Mat Rentals was set up in 1984 and sold in 1989.

Fifth Avenue Food Company was set up in 1988 and in sold in 1994.

Professional Contract Services operated in England and Ireland. Between the two countries, it employed around 2,500 people. The Irish company was sold in 2008; the English one in 2009.

In 2010, Frank and his son Robert, along with Jacky Montgomery, an employee since the age of 15 and now a partner, bought the American Mr Handyman Master Franchise licence for the UK. Currently, all three are all active in growing the Mr Handyman franchise throughout the UK.

Frank's second book – on the family – is written and awaiting publication.

OAK TREE PRESS

Oak Tree Press develops and delivers information, advice and resources for entrepreneurs and managers. It is Ireland's leading business book publisher, with an unrivalled reputation for quality titles across business, management, HR, law, marketing and enterprise topics. NuBooks is its recently-launched imprint, publishing short, focused ebooks for busy entrepreneurs and managers.

In addition, Oak Tree Press occupies a unique position in start-up and small business support in Ireland through its standard-setting titles, as well as training courses, mentoring and advisory services.

Oak Tree Press is comfortable across a range of communication media – print, web and training, focusing always on the effective communication of business information.

Oak Tree Press, 19 Rutland Street, Cork, Ireland.
T: + 353 21 4313855 F: + 353 21 4313496.
E: info@oaktreepress.com
W: www.oaktreepress.com / www.SuccessStore.com.